cp · lot 15ᵘ

THE REGENCY STYLE

THE REGENCY STYLE

1800 TO 1830

By

DONALD PILCHER

*With 150 Illustrations
from Prints, Plans and Photographs*

B. T. BATSFORD, LTD.

LONDON   •   NEW YORK
TORONTO   •   SYDNEY

TO
MY WIFE

First published 1948

*Made and Printed in Great Britain by
Unwin Brothers Ltd., London & Woking
for the Publishers*
B. T. BATSFORD, LTD.
LONDON: 15 North Audley Street, W.1
and MALVERN WELLS, Worcestershire
NEW YORK: 122 East 55th Street
TORONTO: 480–6 University Avenue
SYDNEY: 156 Castlereagh Street

CONTENTS

ACKNOWLEDGMENT

The majority of the illustrations to this book have been taken from photographs and prints in the Publishers' own collection. As regards the remainder, grateful acknowledgment must be made to the following:

Messrs. Aerofilms (Barrats Photo-Press-Agency), for Fig. 127.

The Architects' Journal (The Architectural Press), for Fig. 50.

The late Brian C. Clayton, for Fig. 39.

Messrs. Country Life, Ltd., for Figs. 78 and 131.

Mr. J. Dixon-Scott, F.R.P.S. (The British Council), for Fig. 68.

Mr. Herbert Felton, F.R.P.S., for Figs. 30, 39, 51, 54, 103, 104, 106, 117, 121, 122, 126, 128, 129 and 135.

Miss Frances Hope, for Fig. 51.

Mr. A. F. Kersting, F.R.P.S., for Figs. 15, 76, 116, 119 and 120.

The National Buildings Record, for Figs. 73, 101, 102, 132 and 133.

Mr. Donald Pilcher, A.R.I.B.A., for Figs. 17, 57, 75, 123, 124, 125 and 134.

Mr. Will F. Taylor, for Figs. 69 and 130.

Messrs. Luke Tilley, Ledbury, for Fig. 77.

Messrs. Valentine & Co., for Fig. 71.

The photographs of Stonehouse Victualling Yard on Figs. 101 and 102 have been reproduced by permission of The Admiralty.

The vignette below and that on page 60 are reproduced from Humphry Repton's *Fragments on the Theory and Practice of Landscape Gardening* (1816).

PREFACE

THE period of Regency Architecture is a loosely defined one. The actual years of the Regency may have seen its most characteristic forms. Nevertheless the same forms persist many years after the Regency, while many typical forms were developed during the first decade of the nineteenth century. The truth is that although the Regent, during his years as Regent, may have acted as a sort of patron-in-chief of the Arts, the time was already passing when Royalty exerted much influence on "style" as such. To speak of an "Elizabethan" house or a "William and Mary" chair does imply some connection between those sovereigns and the style evolved under their patronage. A "Regency" table is quite another matter. It may reflect the taste ruling at the Brighton Pavilion: more likely it will not. So that although there was some reflection of the Regent's taste in the architecture of the period there were now (as there had not to any extent been before), other and more popular standards which produced the new building style. The two influences were seldom complementary, and it is in fact by weighing dialectically the one against the other that we can best see how the Regency style was formed. The effect of the "popular" influences, fostered as they were by the Industrial Revolution, become apparent earlier than the change in taste which is expressed by the Regency, so that we have a formative period which dates roughly from the beginning of the century, while the conditions characterising the Regency did not alter materially until the early Victorian years. Nor did the resulting style, so that an overall dating between 1800 and the early 1830s seems to define the period reasonably clearly.

This then is our period. Is it of more than academic interest to us to-day? Certainly it suggests many details of planning and design which are applicable now. In particular, this book, although written before the war, may supplement the *Architectural Review's* recent campaign for "Sharawaggi" in planning. But, beyond this, Regency architecture can help to solve one specific problem which confronts contemporary art. This crucial point has been touched on in a lecture by Herbert Read. "Surely," he says, "between the constructive art of a Gabo or Nicholson, the functional architecture of le Corbusier or Aalto on the one hand, and the rest of what passes for art and architecture on the other hand, there is not merely a separation, but a decree absolute."[1] Ours is, as Mr. Read points out, a "double-decker civilisation" with a geometric, constructive art travelling on the lower deck, and a naturalistic, lyrical art travelling above and with the machine placing a strict ban on fraternisation between the two.

[1] "The Future of Industrial Design." A lecture delivered at the Royal Society under the auspices of the D.I.A., June, 1943.

The Regency top deckers were a self-assertive, jingoistic lot: they had the men, it seems, they had the taste, they had the money too. They were voluble as well, and if we care to read their ideas on architecture we can find them written down with an exuberance and verbosity which has hardly even been paralleled by critics in our own day. We can read and we can see how they established standards of criticism and a vocabulary of design which have largely remained those of popular, one might almost say of philistine art, to this day. This was the naturalistic, sentimental art of the upper deck, but in Regency hands it is hardly ever dull or merely vacuous as it so often is to-day. At the same time there is the geometric, formalised art, already associated with the machine, which, however much it may have become overlaid with naturalistic or sentimental detail, is nevertheless a self-contained art and perhaps the Regency's most serious claim to distinction. Soane may have built himself a "monk's parlour" and Telford designed a castellated bridge "in keeping" with Conway Castle; their art nevertheless remains a spatial, and to some extent a sculptural, adventure which is quite distinct from the romantic trends of the upper deck at this time.

How did these two decks-full of exuberant passengers manage to travel together without overturning the bus? This is Regency Architecture's secret, but if this book manages to throw any light on it, a step will have been taken towards a more homogeneous and effective Modern Architecture.

SALTCOTE,
SOUTH ROAD,
LINDEN EXTENSION,
JOHANNESBURG.

September, 1946.

2 A Shopping Centre: Montpellier Avenue, Cheltenham; and (3) a Fountain at Pittville Spa, Cheltenham

4   The Hyde Park Screen

5   A Regency-Victorian Interior

6   King William in front of the Brighton Pavilion

From "The Cyclopedia of British Costumes" (1828–37)

ARCHITECTURE AS PART OF THE FASHIONABLE BACKGROUND

I

The "Man of Taste"

THE events which decided that there should be a Regency style in architecture will not be found in any history book, and but for the recording pens of Cruikshank and Pierce Egan they might have passed altogether unnoticed. As it is, they have been described for us in the pages of *Life in London*, and illustrated in the pictures of "Corinthian Tom" disporting himself about his "Capital." For included in Tom's make-up as a Georgian aristocrat was that mysterious attribute, the possession of "correct taste," and it was when the "Man of Taste" came to town that the standards of Georgian art emerged in a new guise as those of the Regency. The spectacle of the heir to a Palladian house roystering in Holborn's "Holy Land" in the knowledge that the Philistines are upon him symbolises an important aspect of Regency architecture.

The eighteenth-century "Man of Taste": that self-imposed guide to the grandeur that was Rome, the glory that was Greece and the more obscure preserves of the gloom that was Gothic, had played an important enough part in maintaining the standards of Georgian architecture; but his restraining influence as well as his whimsies had been circumscribed by the limited circle in which he moved. His opinions on the landscape had hardly been headline news, nor had his grottos and his Chinese gardens been the subject of any widespread interest. In the Regency period they were. Such manifestations of Taste were no longer confined to a limited class; they were the hobby of a rapidly widening circle of people.

The difference was one which changing social conditions made inevitable. For at the same time that "Corinthian Tom" was emptying his pockets at the gaming tables of St. James, Alderman Beckford had been filling his in the docks of Poplar. The landed aristocrat had hitherto been the only man in a position to indulge his ideas on architecture, but what with his losses at the gaming tables and the taxes which Mr. Pitt exacted as the price of war, his days as a patron of architecture were already numbered. The time had come when the initiative in architecture, as in so many other things, must pass out of his hands. To the aristocrat as patron, the Regency period added the new class of "clients" of which young Beckford became so spectacular a member. But, in accordance with the much lauded English tradition, it was less in a spirit of self-assertion than of emulating their traditions that the middle classes began to occupy the seats of the ruling aristocracy. Established traditions held their own, and among them the ideal of

B

"Taste" as the mark of cultural distinction. A counterpart to the scramble for wealth, which was to transform the appearance of town and countryside, therefore came to be the scramble for Taste and the expression of its attributes in almost all types of building.

The Regency continued to have its "Arbiters of Taste," the guardians of those rare vintages of which only they could savour the bouquet, but everyone was now determined to sample these rarities for himself. Once he had been primed with a few words from the recognised vocabulary of criticism, he was even prepared to pass judgment on them on his own account. In the effects which it produced, this diffusion of Taste in the Regency period might, not unprofitably, be compared with those occasions on which an indulgent aristocracy caused wine instead of water to flow in the municipal fountains. Had the distributors of these favours themselves partaken of them the parallel would have been even more complete. For some of the ramblings of the Regency aesthete give nothing so much as the impression that he was suffering from the effects of over-indulgence in the more potent of his own vintages. *Enivrer le jardinier, et suivre dans ses pas* was to be put forward as the recipe for designing the landscape garden which was his particular preserve, and the spectacle of his being followed along its "serpentine" path by a host of slightly befuddled admirers is one which provides a not altogether unjust picture of Regency aestheticism. The reservation should however be made that the paths were not altogether of his own making. The directions they were to take had already been determined by previous cultivators of the garden. All that the Regency contributed was the exaggeration of some of their twists and turns and their extension in new, but not altogether unexplored, directions.

For the Georgian period, in which architecture had been so much a matter of conformity to established rules and standards, had also had its outbursts of whimsy. The freedom of the Chinese garden and the rococo interior provided one outlet in this direction. Another, not altogether unconnected with it, was the adventure into emotional associations in architecture. To guide these deviations from the straight and narrow paths of "true taste" and at the same time to keep an eye on "correct" conformity with the classical tradition were the main functions of the "Man of Taste." Above all, he had to keep them in their respective positions: to see that such aesthetic departures should not challenge the standards established in Palladian architecture. Caution was his watchword, and the principle of keeping his definitions of beauty clear of romantic ideas provided a safe method of handling them. Beauty was to be considered a quality apart, a matter of abstract aesthetic values. If the terminology of Bishop Berkeley were adopted, there could be considered to be two distinct kinds of beauty: the "Free Beauty" of direct aesthetic reactions and the "Relative Beauty" of associated ideas.

So with his own house nicely set in order, the eighteenth-century "Man of Taste" had set out to explore those emotional fields which particularly attracted him. In landscapes as yet undisturbed by the "Finger of Taste" he had found the subjects calculated to rouse his emotions, ruined buildings whose obliterated proportions conformed to none of his accepted notions of beauty, but which nevertheless provided a suitable subject for a picture: mountains and forests whose vastness awed him but which possessed none of the attributes of the polished scenery he cultivated. In a ruin he found himself melancholy and reflective, on the battlements of a castle exhilarated but slightly

DRAWING ROOM
From Thomas Hope's *Household Furniture and Interior Decoration* (1807).

apprehensive. Nor was he content until he had replicas of this architecture at his own back door, and until he had elaborated the jargon of the "Sublime" and the "Picturesque" to account for them. "Whether should a ruin be in the Gothic or Grecian form?" asks Lord Kames in his *Elements of Criticism:* "in the former, I think, because it exhibits the triumph of time over strength; a melancholy but not unpleasing thought; a Grecian ruin suggests rather the triumph of barbarity over taste; a gloomy and discouraging thought." Of such a nature were the questions which had occupied the eighteenth-century "Man of Taste" as he busied himself with his garden "improvements."

It is hardly surprising that the less cultivated amateur of the Regency should have got into difficulties when he tried to interpret these emotional niceties on his own account; nor that his garden should often have resembled a sort of cheap edition of the eighteenth-century aristocrat's

estate. It was a pocket estate on these lines that met the astonished gaze
of Lord Colambre as he followed Mrs. Rafferty ("who was determined
to have at least the honour of having a little *taste* of everything at
Tusculum") on a tour of her garden improvements. "She led the way to
a little conservatory, and a little pinery, and a little pheasantry, and a
little dairy for show, and a little cottage for ditto, with a grotto full of
shells, and a little hermitage full of earwigs, and a little ruin full of
looking glass, 'to enlarge and multiply the effect of the Gothic.'—But
you could only put your head in, because it was just fresh painted, and
though there had been a fire ordered in the ruin all night, it had only
smoked."[1] They were brave efforts, these little gestures of faith in aristocratic Taste, and it is a pity that so few of them survived the reformative
zeal of the generation which inherited them. For the plaster and pear-
wood in which most of them seem to have been made were hardly the
materials to stand the searching light of the "Lamp of Truth." It was
only the satirist or the critic of Miss Edgworth's sort who found it
worth while to record them, and such pictures as they have given us
cannot be considered altogether accurate ones. For the middle-class
aspirant to the honours of Taste was not merely fawning on ideas which
he did not understand, as most of his contemporary critics would like
to suggest. His were often honest enough attempts to come to terms
with the aesthetic theories which provided the only cultural standards
he could recognise. If he sometimes fell into such mixtures of "taste
and incongruity, genius and blunder" as Lord Colambre found in the
creations of Mrs. Rafferty, it was probably due less to a cynical mis-
interpretation of the "Man of Taste's" intentions than to that worthy's
setting a pace which was altogether too hot for mere self-made man to
keep up with. The complexity of his theories, added to the fact that
they seldom agreed with those of his rivals, was such that it required a
lifetime of devotion to the cause of Taste if any working principles were
to be deduced from them. Criticism of the "Man of Taste," however,
cuts both ways. It was largely the widespread demand for enlightenment
which accounted for the intricacy of his theories.

In face of this new demand the status of the "Man of Taste" was
considerably modified. He was no longer an "Arbiter" discussing
the merits of rival theories among people familiar with the issues
involved. He had become much more an interpreter of the theories
themselves. Where the eighteenth-century aristocrat had been content
to work out his own salvation in the interpretation of the Sublime and
the Picturesque, this new public could only feel certain that it was on
the "correct" path if it were given exact definitions to follow and established models to imitate. Where Addison's hint that "a man might make
a pretty landskip of his own possessions" had provided a sufficient
incentive for readers of the *Spectator* to start exploring the picturesque
possibilities of their grounds, Humphry Repton had to write volumes
explaining exactly how they should set about it. In the same way the

[1] Maria Edgworth: *The Absentee.*

7   Grecian for the elegance of the Pastrycook

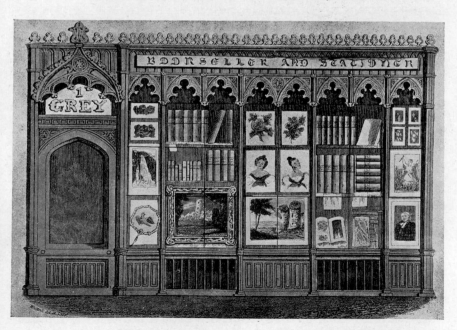

8   Gothic for the "Sublime" Prints of the Bookseller

From "Shopfronts of London"

TASTE IN SHOPFRONT DESIGN

9　The Theatre Royal, Drury Lane. *Benjamin Wyatt, Architect* (1811–12)

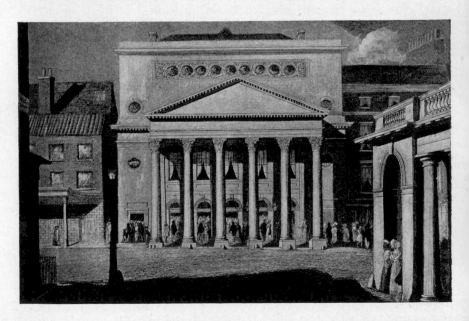

10　The New Theatre Royal, Haymarket. *John Nash, Architect* (1820–1)

From "The Theatres of London," by Daniel Havell (1826)

THE REGENCY THEATRE

Regency amateur could not be content with the mere principles of "The Painters" as models for the Picturesque, as his eighteenth-century forerunner had been. He had to be told exactly which painters to admire and which aspects of their compositions to imitate. It was largely in response to this demand for definite models that the convenient theory was produced that the garden should copy actual pictures by approved landscape painters.

The chief result of these attempts to discover exactly what was Picturesque seem to have been the discovery that there was very little that was not. Thus Payne Knight, when he embarks on a catalogue of recommended subjects, finds it necessary to add copiously to those accepted by the eighteenth century. In his *Analytical Enquiry into The Principles of Taste* the "warriors of Salvator Rosa, the apostles of Raphael and the bacchanalians of Poussin" march in ragged ranks beside "the boors of Ostade, the peasants of Gainsborough, and the shepherds of Bergen": and in the same Picturesque procession "The pampered warhorse with luxuriant mane and flowing tail, which we so justly admire in the pictures of Wovermans" prances beside its contemporary counterpart, "the shaggy worn-out hack or cart horse of Morland." Of greater moment for the landscape garden, is the planting of "the giant oak of Ruysdael, or the full grown pine or ilex of Claude" in the same scene as the "stumpy decayed Pollard of Rubens or Rembrandt." The Regency enormously increased the scope of the Picturesque, but the Italian school admired by the eighteenth century remained the point of departure. The well-known clause in Turner's will, asking that his pictures should be hung beside Claude's, shows how even so revolutionary a painter continued to judge his work by their standards.

But while such catalogues as Payne Knight's might be considered as providing useful enough information for the uninitiated, he would feel still more confident of his ability to judge matters of Taste if he knew which subjects should be considered more Picturesque than others. Hence Payne Knight's attempts to distinguish different degrees of picturesqueness in the subjects he enumerates. "The dirty and tattered garments, the dishevelled hair, and general wild appearance of gipsies and beggar girls," in his opinion, "are picturesque," but the "flowing ringlets, fine shawls, and robes of delicate muslin thrown into all the easy, negligent, and playful folds of antique drapery by polished grace and refined elegance are still more so." Similarly in architecture: "The mouldering ruins of ancient temples, theatres and aqueducts, enriched by such variety of tints, all mellowed into each other, as they appear in the landscapes of Claude, are, in the highest degree, picturesque; but the magnificent quays and palaces adorned with porticos and balustrades, and intermixed with shipping, which enrich the seaports of the same master, are likewise picturesque, though in a less degree."[1] In such passages we can already see preliminary skirmishes of the coming "battle of the Styles."

[1] Payne Knight: *Analytical Enquiry.*

C

Definitions of the Picturesque and descriptions of its attributes might have been of more use if a sufficient number of the authorities had managed to agree about them. As it was, few of them ever did manage to agree, and a considerable amount of time which might have been better employed was spent in slinging mud at the idols set up by their rivals. Payne Knight, for example, joins issue with Sir Uvedale Price on the burning question as to whether the squint of the parson's daughter ". . . made upon the model of her father's house" ("her features are as irregular, and her eyes are inclined to look across each other, like the roofs of the old parsonage. . .") was sufficient claim to Picturesque quality (and in Price's eyes adequate grounds for matrimony) or whether, to complete the picture satisfactorily, "the same happy mixture of the irregular and the Picturesque must have prevailed through her limbs and person; and consequently she must have hobbled as well as squinted; and had hips and shoulders as irregular as her teeth, cheeks and eyebrows."[1]

With the same gusto and a similar lack of useful conclusions they attack the even more sticky subject of the Sublime, in the course of which battle Price again comes in for some hard knocks from Knight. His parallel between the *terrible* cattle of the Newmarket Drovers and the equivalent use of the word by Aristotle and Longinus is, for example, summarily dealt with by the reminder that "My friend Mr. Price . . . might also have heard . . . of some persons being *damned* clever, and others *damned stupid*." In fact Payne Knight shows scant respect either for his rival, Price, or for its original analyst, Burke, when it comes to defining the attributes of the Sublime. But while there is no reason to doubt Payne Knight's statement that he "had never met with any man of learning by whom the philosophy of the *Inquiry into the Sublime and the Beautiful* was not as much despised and ridiculed, as the brilliancy and animation of its style was applauded and admired," Burke's were nevertheless some of the most commonly discussed theories of the time. For this immature treatise, which he himself denounced in later life, had introduced many ideas which fitted neatly into the moods cultivated by the Regency romantics. The "sort of delightful horror, a sort of tranquillity tinged with terror," which Burke had decided was one of its main ingredients, was, for instance, a consoling definition of the "Weltschmerz" which haunted men who, like Peacock's "Scythrop," slept "with horrid mysteries under his pillow, and dreamed of venerable eleutherarchs and ghastly confederates holding midnight conventions in subterranean caves."[2] On a more material plane, the inclusion of prodigious antiquity and terrific size as Sublime attributes lent a measure of respectability to the suggestions of these qualities which appeared in the houses of the newly rich. But, as in the case of the Picturesque, attempts to catalogue examples and to give exact definitions of the Sublime finished in nothing more conclusive than an inextricable tangle of words. Even if it were possible to appreciate the all-important

---

[1] Payne Knight: *Analytical Enquiry.*   [2] Thomas Love Peacock: *Nightmare Abbey.*

11   "An Ornamental Cottage and Ruins," by Robert Lugar (1815)

12   "A Picturesque Dairy"

From "The Repository of Arts, Literature and Fashion" (Jan. 1821)

DESIGNS ACCORDING TO "LEFT-WING" THEORIES OF THE
PICTURESQUE

13   A typical Regency Interior with French Window opening on to the Ground.
The Drawing-room at Bromley Hall, Kent (1816)

14 A Formal Interior

From a painting by W. Pickett (1811)

distinction between the *pleasure* and *delight* occasioned by a terrifying spectacle, there still remained such problems to be solved as the one presented by Payne Knight, as to ". . . whether the dog who fought against the murderers of his master, and, after being mortally wounded in his defence, lay two days by his lifeless body, and then expired in attempting to seize one of the persons who took it up, is an object of more true sublimity, than a wolf worrying a sheep, or a lion or tiger springing from the covert of a thicket upon their unsuspecting prey."[1] The hint which the author gives in a footnote that "Lions and tigers, like all other animals of the cat kind, are cowardly and treacherous; and never openly face an enemy, but always attack by surprise," is not one which seems to throw much light on the solution.

Under the circumstances it is understandable enough that it should be less the "Man of Taste" himself than the journalist and the popular novelist, serving up versions of his theories in a more palatable form, whose inside information on Taste was more confidently followed. It was both easier, and for the untutored mind, more informative, to read Francis Jeffrey's essays in the *Edinburgh Review* than to read the original ideas behind them in the *Principles of Taste* by Jeffrey's lodging-house acquaintance, Archibald Alison. Similarly, it was infinitely more entertaining to have the "Gothic magnificence of Udolpho" described through eyes as responsive to the Sublime as were those of Mrs. Radcliffe's Emily, than to seek enlightenment in Burke's *Philosophical Enquiry* into its *Origins*. Mrs. Radcliffe, who had sat at the feet of "Athenian" Stewart, could be considered as reliable an authority as any when it came to interpreting mysteries so Eleusinian in their obscurity as those of the Sublime and the Beautiful. For to her contemporaries *The Mysteries of Udolpho* was not only an exciting adventure story. It was no less an informative commentary on architecture and landscape. And beside Mrs. Radcliffe was a host of writers on the same pattern. Their novels, which provided the "popular" reading of the day, have been given the collective title of the "Gothic Romances." Although many of them were published well before the end of the eighteenth century, it was during the Regency years that they were most prolific, while their sentiments remained much the same as those of the earlier examples. Jane Austen, who satirised them in *Northanger Abbey*, and Scott, who made some pointed allusions to them in the preface of *Waverley*, had replaced them on the counters of the lending library before the Regency period had run its course.

Waverley itself illustrates the difference between the "Gothic Romance" and the Victorian novel which followed it: how Scott's descriptions of architecture are used to define the characters, instead of being mere descriptions for their own sake, in the tradition of the Regency novel. The "Gothic Romance" was in fact following the same impulses as the eighteenth-century "Man of Taste." Its characters were concerned, if anything, more with orientating themselves to their

[1] Payne Knight: *Analytical Enquiry.*

surroundings than to each other. For a complete picture of any age we must look to its journalism and to its popular literature, as well as to the more worthy literature which has survived, and in the case of the Regency this is particularly true, for the "Gothic Romances" show us the extent to which aesthetic theory had been assimilated by the people who read them. Take, for example, such characters as Ethelinde (*The Recluse of the Lake*) who, "Sitting down on a rustic and half ruined tomb . . . contemplated with mournful pleasure the Picturesque appearance it made adjoining the church,"[1] or the character from *The Vicar of Lansdowne*, with his observation that "the fine old ruin impresses the mind with the most pleasing, the most awful, the most soothing sensations."[2] Here are direct reflections of contemporary "Taste"; of its preoccupation with the Picturesque, and in the "awful" and "soothing" effects of the ruin, a reference to the "restrained terror" which was considered a necessary ingredient of the Sublime. Such tastes, which had been the exclusive prerogative of the eighteenth-century aristocrat, had become, by way of the popular novel, almost the commonplaces of Regency conversation. Catherine Morland, with her expectations of Udolpho Sublimity from every mediaeval house, and Marianne Dashwood who, when faced with a Picturesque prospect, sometimes kept her "feelings" to herself "because I could find no language to describe them in but what was worn and hackneyed out of all meaning,"[3] were typical products of the "Sensibility" emulated in the "Gothic Romance." Considering the transports of Taste in which some of their heroines indulged, a little more of Marianne's sense would clearly not have been out of place. For to a properly cultivated Sensibility the merest architectural details could become charged with Sublime significance. In one case a mere glimpse of a pitched roof is sufficient. This "peaked roof," we are told, ". . . half lost in air, and half, by straining her sight, kept in view, excited mingled passions—a sensation of terror and delight."[4] Even the drawing-room windows were apparently capable of striking terror into susceptible bosoms, for, in another case, young ladies are found protesting that "unless the dark Gothic windows and hideous tapestry were removed from the drawing room, and light sashes substituted in their stead, they should fall into hysterics every time they went into the room."[5]

It was only to be expected that this literary approach to architecture should tend to exploit the more outrageous of the notions of contemporary critics. But such excess of aesthetic zeal was not likely to have widespread effects on the architecture of the time. What is more important about these novels is that they helped to make the discussion of architecture and landscape something of a fashionable pastime among the people who read them. In *Udolpho* they could read of Emily's wanderings round the castle walls; of how "the grandeur of the broad

[1] Mrs. Smith: *Ethelinde.*   [2] Mrs. Roche: *The Vicar of Lansdowne.*
[3] Jane Austen: *Sense and Sensibility.*   [4] Mrs. Roche: *Treconthick Bower.*
[5] Mrs. West: *A Tale of the Times.*

ramparts, and the changing scenery they overlooked, excited her high admiration; for the extent of the terraces allowed the features of the country to be seen in such various points of view, that they appeared to form new landscapes." Passages such as this, appearing not in an abstruse aesthetic treatise but in a best-selling novel, and repeated, as they were, *ad nauseam* in less successful imitations, could not fail to have some effect on the people who read them. From discussing Mrs. Radcliffe's descriptions of the Pyrenees over the tea-cups they inevitably came to discuss the more familiar landscape of their own countryside and the buildings in it. Hence the walks, picnics and excursions to neighbouring ruins which play such an important part in Jane Austen's novels. Often they went further afield. Encouraged by Gilpin's descriptions of the English countryside they set out to see these beauties for themselves, and to pass judgment on them in terms with which the lending library had already made them familiar.

The popular novel taught numbers of people to look at their surroundings in a way in which they had never looked before. It taught them above all to criticise them not in aesthetic but in literary terms. The heroine of the "Gothic Romance," perpetually menaced and bullied as she was by her architectural surroundings, had neither the opportunity nor, to read between the lines, the ability to appreciate real aesthetic values. And so it tended to be with her imitators. The Taste of the Regency, as it came to be interpreted by the "reading public" in their new and more formidable guise as architect's clients, was a matter not so much of planning and proportion as of suggesting an approved emotion. They imitated to the best of their ability the architecture which their novel-reading recommended to them, but they imitated it not so much for its architectural qualities as for its literary ones.

This attitude was one which might have had more serious effects on architecture if a practical interpretation of it had been easier. As it was, the difficulties were considerable. For, from the literary point of view, the ideal house was, if not a complete ruin, at least a building so structurally unsound as to be quite uninhabitable. It was actually the construction of a sort of habitable ruin, which was the original idea behind Beckford's "Folly" at Fonthill, but there were few other people in a position to indulge in such an extravagant fancy. The devotees of the Sublime in general had to be content with a more modest reminder of melancholy and "restrained terror" in their houses, and a few crockets and battlements, with their associations of Gothic gloom, would generally suffice for the purpose. And there was always the consideration that, however much the Sublime was to be admired at a picnic outing to the local ruins, it was hardly a desirable quality to have always about the house. The Sublime, if it were to be domesticated at all, was better left out in the garden. If it were allowed into the house occasionally, it was confined to such an obscure corner as the one to which Sir John Soane relegated it when he made the "Monks' Parlour" in his house in Lincoln's Inn Fields.

The true romantic spirit seems in fact to have decided that the proper
setting for his moods was not one to construct but one to fashion out
of existing material. Some, as Byron did at Newstead, managed to find
the setting they required ready-made in their own houses. Others had
to go further afield. Lady Hester Stanhope, after calling in the Dover
garrison to pull Pitt's castle at Walmer into reasonably romantic shape,
eventually migrated to a collection of shacks on Mount Lebanon,
where she was able to practise "restrained terror" in face of imminent
danger from the hostile Arabs. There were, however, other attributes
of the Sublime which could be better adapted to the limitations of
architects and clients. In the garden a good deal could be done by a
judicious shaping of the landscape, and, in his magnificent rides at
Bayham Abbey, Repton managed to enforce the canons of Sublimity
even in so unpromising a setting as the Kentish countryside. Much
too could be done by selecting a suitable site for a house. Perched on
the edge of a beetling cliff or rocky promontory even a stucco villa
could acquire something of Sublimity, and the series of romantic
drawings made by Robert Adam in 1782 must have provided useful
hints as to how this could be done. Piranesi also suggested some
effective precedents and young Beckford, whose towers were later to
materialise in the less sublime landscapes of Salisbury and Bath,
invoked his drawings as he drove down the Rhine Valley . . . and
"mounted on fantastic quadrupeds, I shot from rock to rock and built
castles in the style of Piranesi upon most of their pinnacles. The
magnificence and variety of my aerial towers hindered my thinking the
way long." For the importance of having towers was recognised by all
true devotees of the Sublime. "Why is it so sublime," asks Mrs. Radcliffe, "to stand at the foot of a dark tower, and look up its height to
the sky and stars?"[1] The same thought inspired a crop of mansions in
the "castellated" and kindred styles.

Another important attribute of the Sublime was its associations with
"Antiquity." It was one which, in view of the trend of the times, could
not fail to have effects on architecture. Like its other attributes it
played particularly into the hands of the Gothic revivalists. The
opportunity it gave of flaunting his coat of arms must have played no
small part in Beckford's decision to adopt the Gothic style at
Fonthill (18), and the same idea produced a more modest display of
crockets on the villas of his imitators. William Cobbett, with his
honest yeoman disgust at the pretensions of the rising middle class,
found a fit subject for his invective in a house of this sort which he
encountered on his "Rural Rides." He had been rude enough about
Beckford's coats of arms ("The negro-driver brag of his high blood"),
but this unfortunate Mr. Montague suffers even greater contempt for
his Gothic house and the "mock-magnificence" of the landscape
garden which went with it. "I do not know who this gentleman is,"
he rants, "I suppose that he is some honest person from the 'Change'

[1] *Gaston de Blondeville.*

15   A Characteristic Design in Stucco by John Nash.   York Gate, Regent's Park (*c.* 1822)

16 Fonthill Abbey: The Hall

17 The Tower of Hadlow, Kent: a later addition to a Regency House

18 Fonthill Abbey: the Exterior
From the "Illustrated History and Description," by John Rutter (1823)

ESSAYS IN THE SUBLIME

or its neighbourhood, and that these GOTHIC ARCHES are to denote the ANTIQUITY OF HIS ORIGIN." By building a house in the Gothic style, or by grafting a row of battlements on to their suburban villas, the middle classes were able to assert at the same time their sensibility to the Sublime and, like Mr. Montague, their claim to a respectable antiquity. And, as the Regency dilettante was not a man to do things

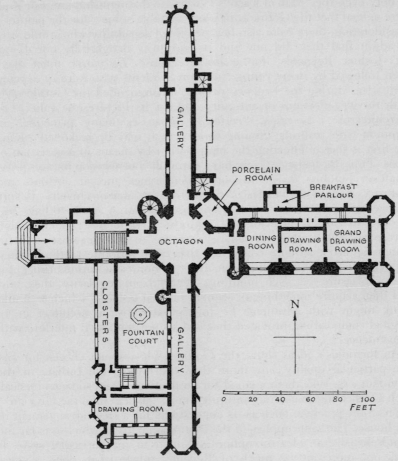

PLAN OF FONTHILL ABBEY

by halves, there was many an owner of a Gothic mansion who rounded off such architectural gestures by adopting a name with a suitably Gothic flavour. The father of Thackeray's Sir Alured de Mogyns came a step nearer to "antiquity" when he dropped the name of plain Mr. Muggins, and, in the same strain, a family already distinguished in the architectural profession acquired a new dignity when, after completing his additions to Windsor Castle, Mr. Jeffry Wyatt was transformed into the more Sublime figure of "Sir Jeffry Wyattville."

But while these associations provided many practical motives for reviving the Gothic style, a more important consideration was its Picturesque quality. The finding of watertight compartments for its aesthetic theories was a heritage from eighteenth-century Taste which the Regency took considerable trouble to live up to, but in Gothic architecture the Sublime and the Picturesque were so intermingled as to defy even the "Man of Taste's" efforts to distinguish them. For if all were agreed that the Gothic ruin was a suitable subject for the painter's consideration, there were also few people of sensibility who would care to admit that they did not find its antiquity delightfully horrifying. Sir Joshua Reynolds, for example, whose *Discourses* must have been followed by many young Academy students who were to develop their ideas during the Regency period, recommended the Gothic style both for its reflections of antiquity and for its Picturesque value. For "Architecture," he says, "certainly possesses many principles in common with painting. Among those which may be reckoned among the first is that of affecting the imagination by means of association of ideas. Thus, for instance, as we have naturally a veneration for antiquity, whatever building brings to our remembrance ancient customs and manners, such as the castles of the Barons of ancient chivalry, is sure to give this delight. . . . For this purpose Vanburgh seems to have had recourse to some of the principles of Gothic Architecture; which though not so ancient as the Grecian, is more so to our imagination, with which the artist is more concerned than with absolute truth. It often happens that additions have been made to houses at various times, for use or pleasure. As such buildings depart from regularity, they now and then acquire something of scenery on that account, which I should think might with advantage be incorporated by an architect in an original composition, provided that it does not too much interfere with convenience."

As Reynolds's ideas show, the Gothic style was not chosen for any one particular quality, any more than the Greek, the Indian, or the Egyptian was. Like them it stood for a variety of ideas: some whimsical, such as reflecting an abstract antiquity more "ancient than the Grecian"; others more practical, such as its suggestions for a freer arrangement of the house. The same applies to the Picturesque itself, which was far too comprehensive an idea to confine architects to any particular style. It does not represent, as much of Regency romanticism does, a mere hankering after literary associations. It has a deeper aesthetic significance which runs all through Regency architecture, and distinguishes it, more than anything else, from its Georgian prototype. From the interiors of Soane to the town-planning of Nash, Picturesque principles distinguish almost the whole of Regency architecture. Price and his disciples certainly made efforts to limit it to the type of painting which they particularly admired, but their ideas got little sympathy from architects. J. B. Papworth, for example, states the architect's view of the Picturesque when, in reply to Price's assertion that "the two opposite qualities of roughness and of sudden variations joined to that of irregularity are the most efficient causes of the Picturesque," he writes that ". . . The fundamental error has arisen out of the too common opinion that all which is not rugged and rude is not Picturesque; whereas beauty and fitness are its indispensable characteristics, it exists wherever these qualities are combined, and ceases where they are not."[1] His conclusions, like those of most of Regency architects where the word "fitness" is involved, are more than a little vague, but his main intention is clear enough; and it is representative of architectural

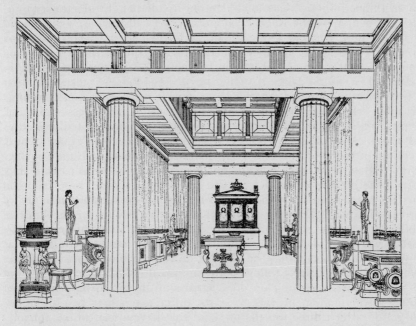

A STATUE GALLERY
From Thomas Hope's *Household Furniture and Interior Decoration* (1807).

opinion. Whatever concessions might be made to other associations; whether the final results of the architect's labours turned out to be Indian, Moorish, Gothic or Greek, or just straightforward architecture, it is his appreciation of the formal values of the Picturesque which gives his buildings the quality which we associate with the Regency.

Much of Regency architecture was, as has already been pointed out, only a wider application of ideas that had been experimented with on a modest scale by the eighteenth-century "Man of Taste." This is particularly true in the case of the Picturesque. The principles of composition which had been applied to the layout of the eighteenth-century garden were, during the Regency period, adapted to the layout of town parks and housing estates: even to the design of streets. Regent

[1] J. B. Papworth: *Ornamental Gardening* (1823).

D

Street owed as much to Picturesque principles as Regent's Park.
Meanwhile eighteenth-century experiments in designing buildings with
an eye to the landscapes in which they stood developed into the
characteristic Regency house. Picturesque principles determined its
exterior form, its interior planning, even its decorative detail. The same
applies, to a limited extent, to the town house and to the design and
layout of monumental buildings.

The danger of such a widespread enthusiasm for the Picturesque
was that it should be cultivated to the exclusion of mere "beauty";
in fact that literary ideas should come to detract from standards of
design. If more of the Regency amateurs had had their way this would
certainly have happened. As it was, architects on the whole managed
to satisfy the rising clamour for the Picturesque without conceding
too much in the way of architectural principles. "Are not new buildings
beautiful?" asks Payne Knight, pondering Price's statement that
"Buildings are moulded out of Beauty into Picturesqueness"; "Unques-
tionably," he concludes, "they are. For neatness, freshness, lightness,
symmetry, regularity, uniformity and propriety are undoubtedly beauties
of the highest class."[1] Coming from an "Arbiter of Taste" whose
reputation was sufficient to survive his assertion that the Elgin Marbles
were Roman work, such a statement is reassuring. However much they
may have become embroiled in the literary onslaught, these men did
in fact manage to keep their taste for the more substantial body of
architecture comparatively unimpaired. To read between the lines of
their aesthetic tracts it would even seem that the manœuvrings in the
battle were considered more important than the issues involved. Was
it by chance or design that the chapter on the Sublime in the *Principles
of Taste* is immediately followed by one on the *Ridiculous*? And what
of the author's summing up on what might appear to be a matter of
grave aesthetic moment, that ". . . the difference is merely a difference
of words, which three-fourths of those that have arisen in metaphysics
and moral philosophy, as well as in religion, have been; and as long
as the disputes concerning them are confined to the shedding of ink,
and do not extend to the shedding of blood, they afford a very innocent
amusement to the several disputants, of which I am now enjoying the
benefit."[2] In short, it might be put forward as the saving grace of
Regency aestheticism that the participants in its battle were men of
far too wide a culture to pin their faith on any set of rules as such.
It was the converted Philistine, the subscriber to the lending library,
who needed rules and classified ideas as a substitute for a Taste he
was only too conscious of not possessing. The true "Man of Taste"
seems to have appreciated clearly enough that architecture cannot live
by theory alone and that the words he used were merely convenient
terms for defining general aesthetic trends. The Picturesque was such
a trend and it was the one particularly characteristic of Regency architecture. Perhaps its nature will be easier to appreciate if we compare

[1] Payne Knight: *Analytical Enquiry*.   [2] Ibid.

19   A *Cottage Ornée*

20   "A *Cottage Ornée*, designed for the neighbourhood of the Lakes."

Both from "Rural Residences" (1818)

RUSTIC DESIGNS BY J. B. PAPWORTH

21　The Holme, Regent's Park.　*Decimus Burton, Architect*
From "Metropolitan Improvements" (1831)

22　Proposed Entrance Lodge to Bayham
From "Designs for Lodges and Entrances," by J. D. W. Dearn (1811)

SCENERY CONSIDERED APPROPRIATE FOR "GRECIAN" AND
"GOTHIC" HOUSES

it with the tendency of modern architects to think of their buildings in terms of their photographic value. The ultimate aim of much Regency architecture was that it should look well as a steel engraving, just as much modern architecture is designed with an eye to its appearance in an illustrated periodical. Both are liable to criticism on this account, but both acquire distinctive merits through the point of view which they adopt.

Perhaps the greatest achievement of the Picturesque was the com-

AN INTERIOR
From Henry Moses' *Designs of Modern Costume* (1823).

pleteness with which it rounded off its buildings. They were not only carefully related to their surroundings; they were no less designed with an eye to the people who used them. The sense of "congruity" was a recognised term in architectural criticism; and it accounts not only for such random fancies as the retaining of a blind harper by the Earl of Shrewsbury to inhabit a "Rustic" cottage on his estate, it accounts no less for the sense of completeness which runs all through Regency design. When, in conformity with Picturesque principles, houses went Greek or Gothic, so did the people who lived in them. Its devotee who built himself a Gothic tower adopted the monkish habit along with his architecture. The Picturesque of the Regency amateur was on a plane altogether different from that of his modern counterpart whose rafters ring with the strains of the Jacobean radio. Ladies in dresses designed on Gothic lines who looked up at the Gothic

battlements of their houses were thinking what they fondly imagined to
be Gothic thoughts. Their sisters in Greek draperies, seated on Greek
chairs and drinking tea brewed in Greek urns, were endeavouring to

AN INTERIOR

From Henry Moses' *Designs of Modern Costumes* (1823).

comport themselves with a dignity which they equally fondly imagined
to be Greek. Whatever we may think of the Regency's essays in the
Picturesque we must at least appreciate the picture it has left us of
an age living, as none has done since, in harmony with its architectural
background.

II

The Landscape Garden and its Influence

IF there was one point on which all Regency "Men of Taste" were agreed it was that in any discussion on aesthetics Nature must have the last word. It was to her that they finally appealed to settle their disputes, and it was in the "natural," or landscape, garden that they cultivated their theories. The result was that the *furor hortensis* continued to rage as fiercely during the Regency period as it had done in Lord Chesterfield's day, while the special form it took is recorded by Peacock's Mr. Milestone, who reserved "the noble art of picturesque gardening" for "the exclusive genius of the present times."[1] Even if the Picturesque gardener could not justifiably claim as Mr. Milestone did, to have given "a new outline to the physiognomy of the universe," he could at least boast that his ideas had affected landscapes far removed from the English countryside. It was not long since Voltaire had been advising his readers to cultivate their gardens, and Catherine for one had responded by planning hers on the lines of *le jardin anglais*. Many of her contemporaries could have written to Voltaire, as she did, describing how ". . . *a present l'anglomanie domine dans ma plantomanie*":[2] and in the same tradition Papworth and the Reptons were, during the Regency, laying out gardens as far afield as Holland, Germany and Portugal. But while the English landscape was being welcomed abroad, its sponsors at home were standing trial on the all-important issue of the Picturesque. The layout of the landscape garden provided a test case for current aesthetic theories and the verdicts given enormously affected the architecture which was implicated in it. As such the garden provides the best viewpoints from which to study the Regency house.

One thing which the Regency "Men of Taste" managed to make abundantly clear was their dissatisfaction with the prevailing school of gardening, while, such was the nature of the Picturesque, that the house which went with it could scarcely avoid its share of unfavourable comments. For while Littlebrain Castle, that "white, polished, angular building, its contours reflected to a nicety in the waveless lake below"[3] is, in a sense, typical of the Regency house and its setting, most of the leading "Men of Taste" were agreed that the Picturesque was capable of better things. The poet Mason, an earlier critic of the "natural"

[1] Peacock: *Headlong Hall.*   [2] Catherine the Great: *Letters to Voltaire.*
[3] Peacock: *Headlong Hall.*

17

garden, who saw in "Capability" Brown's layouts "rather traces of
the kitchen gardener of Old Stowe than of Poussin or Claude Lorraine,"
had proposed as a remedy that ". . . Gainsborough gave the design and
Brown executed"; and a similar conformity with the principles of
"The Painters" was suggested by Price and Payne Knight as a means
of "improving" the eighteenth-century garden. Price in his garden at
Foxley, in which he interpreted the intricacies catalogued in his *Essay
on the Picturesque*, and Payne Knight in his at Downton, where he
cultivated the beauties described in his poem on *The Landscape*,
illustrated their respective ideas on how the "picture gardener" should
set to work.

The "paper battle"which revolved round the merits of these gardens
is a subject of more than literary interest, for it represents an essential
phase in the war which overthrew the reigning Palladian house and
in its place set up the loose federation of the Regency "styles." To
follow all its intricacies would involve a treatise as tedious as are many
of the expositions of the Picturesque themselves. One particular aspect
of it should however be borne in mind, namely that, as in the case of
most wars, it started by pinning its faith in one cause and finished
by espousing another. A war which was fought in the name of a more
Picturesque form of gardening ended by establishing a more formal
one. Another complicating factor is the fact that the "paper battle"
was a three-cornered contest. The chief antagonists, Payne Knight and
Sir Uvedale Price, are already familiar figures. The third was Humphry
Repton, the leading landscape gardener practising in the eighteenth-
century tradition.

It was above all the threat to freedom of action in the landscape
garden which induced Repton to join issue in the "paper battle."
Because the "natural" garden had become as stereotyped in treatment
as was the formal garden against which it had originally revolted, its
critics saw fit to condemn the whole art of landscape gardening as it
was practised at the time, threatening to set up in its place dictatorships
founded on their separate philosophies of landscape painting. As an
arch traitor to the cause of the "natural" garden they pilloried Capability
Brown: "Thy favourite Brown," as Payne Knight describes him in his
poem on *The Landscape*,

> . . . whose innovating hand
> First dealt out curses o'er this fertile land,
> First taught the walks in spiral forms to move
> And from their haunts the secret Dryads drove . . .

Certainly Brown's rule-of-thumb methods laid him open to criticism.
Even more so did those of the men contemptuously described by Repton
as the "day-labourers who became his successors." Under these victims
of the *furor hortensis* everything was banished from the garden which
failed to conform to Burke's notion of polished beauty or Hogarth's
recipe of the "serpentine line." The resulting ". . . system of levelling,

23   A "View from the Private Apartments'

24   The "West Front, towards the Garden"

From "Designs for the Pavilion at Brighton" (1806)

GARDEN TREATMENTS SUGGESTED BY REPTON FOR THE BRIGHTON PAVILION

25, 26   Repton's suggestions for Shardeloes Park before and after
"Improvement"

From "Observations on the Theory and Practice of Landscape Gardening" (1805)

THE LANDSCAPE GARDEN AND ITS INFLUENCE

and trimming, and clipping, and docking, and clumping, and polishing and shaving"[1] was not only one which, in the view of so well-versed an authority on Uvedale Price as Sir Patrick O'Prism, destroyed "all the beautiful intricacies of natural luxuriance, and all the graduated harmonies of light and shade, melting into one another": it represented no less what Knight described as a "sacrifice of feeling for system" which was clearly incompatible with any attempt to handle the landscape in a "natural" way.

There were plenty of Regency enthusiasts for Brown's school of gardening who, like Mrs. Rafferty, "hated everything straight, it was so formal and unpicturesque." There were also plenty of his imitators who were guilty of the rather indelicate assault on the presiding deity of the landscape described by Payne Knight as ". . . shaving the goddess whom they came to dress":[2] but such misplaced zeal was hardly sufficient justification for condemning the Brown landscape, lock, stock and barrel. At least that was the view held by Repton, who, although he was not above questioning some of Brown's "Capabilities," styled himself a follower of his principles and stood the fire of the picture-gardeners' criticism on that account.

Nor did Repton prove such an easy target as the picture-gardeners imagined. In the literary mêlée he was certainly at a disadvantage, and fair game for such thrusts as Payne Knight's distinction between *elegans formarum spectator* and *elegantiae formarum spectator*.[3] But, when it came to more practical issues, Repton's level-headedness and practical knowledge of his subject proved more than a match for their dilettanti view of the landscape. Instead of a timid literary hare they found that they had started so monstrous an architectural crow that this aesthetic Tweedledum and Tweedledee quite forgot their own quarrel. The cause of the battle was in any case less important than its effect in bringing the principles of landscape gardening more into the light of day. Malton's is the final verdict on it when he says that ". . . from the literary controversy that has taken place between these gentlemen, and from the spirit with which it has been conducted, myself and the public are put in possession of many valuable precepts and hints, which, but for it, we might probably never have possessed."[4]

For, as the acknowledged master of an art which was also a popular craze, Repton not only had to defend principles which were being attacked by men far better versed than he was in the niceties of aesthetic controversy. He also had to endure being made the scapegoat for the sins of the flock of fashionable "improvers" which he was supposed to represent. "I saw myself," he says, "attacked in the public papers for blunders at places I had never visited or for absurdities introduced at places before I visited them; and I heard opinions quoted as mine, which I had never advanced and was blamed for errors I had never advised."[5]

[1] Peacock: *Headlong Hall.*   [2] Payne Knight: *The Landscape.*
[3] Ibid.: *Analytical Enquiry.*   [4] James Malton: *Designs for Villas* (1802).
[5] J. Loudon: *Biographical Notice of the Late Humphry Repton, Esq.*

His grievance was a legitimate one. It is immortalised in *Headlong Hall*. In it the character of "Mr. Milestone" is immediately identifiable as Repton by way of the latter's discussion with Payne Knight on the desirability of a gentleman's setting up milestones to suggest "the extent of his property." (Repton, as Peacock recalls in a footnote, insisted that he said "mere stones" and not "milestones.") The way in which Mr. Milestone proposes to remedy the fact that Squire Headlong's grounds "had never been touched by the finger of Taste" is the last one that Repton himself would have chosen. "My dear sir," he asks, "accord me your permission, to wave the wand of enchantment over your grounds. The rocks shall be blown up, the trees shall be cut down, the wilderness and all its goats shall vanish like mist. Pagodas and Chinese bridges, gravel walks and shrubberies, bowling-greens, canals, and clumps of larch shall rise upon its ruins."

Nor is Peacock the only offender in this respect. Another is Jane Austen, who attributes to Repton the intention of felling the avenue at Mansfield Park. "Mr. Repton," decides Mr. Rushworth, "or anybody of that sort would certainly have the avenue down"; while Fanny Price's invocation of Cowper's

> . . . fallen avenues,
> Once more I mourn your fate unmerited . . .

is met with smiling indulgence and the affirmation, "I am afraid the avenue stands a bad chance, Fanny."[1] Such were the "unjust imputations" which Repton had to endure from the novelists as well as from more ephemeral critics. For, when he waved his "wand of enchantment," the trees did not necessarily group themselves into belts and clumps, nor was the avenue necessarily doomed to an unmerited fate. Unlike many of his fellow landscapists he did not disapprove of avenues as avenues, but only when they blocked a prospect by cutting across the view. Even then the avenue, contrary to Mr. Rushworth's accusation, stood a good chance, for Repton's general remedy was to remove a few trees so as to open up a prospect through it, while not spoiling the effect of the avenue along its length. The justness of his observations on this account can still be appreciated in such landscapes as the one in Langley Park, where he suggested an "improvement" on these lines.

A proper appreciation of Repton's work is in fact hampered by his being a sort of dual personality. To most of his contemporaries he was an elusive figure in a coach flitting from one subject of "improvement" to another. Wherever a garden took the shape of the fashionable trimmed landscape the finger of the Reptonian taste was, often unjustifiably, detected. Similarly, gardens for which he suggested improvements which never materialised, or in which they were carried out in a very half-hearted manner, are still criticised as being "Repton gardens." It was therefore not altogether a hankering after the amateur status from which he had fallen, as the result of unsuccessful speculation in

[1] Jane Austen: *Mansfield Park.*

27 House, Park and Ornamental Water designed, by Repton, as a single composition, in his sketch for Bayham

From "Observations on the Theory and Practice of Landscape Gardening" (1805)

28   No. 13 Woburn Place, London

29   The Bedford Hotel, Sidmouth

TENT FORMS AND TRELLIS APPLIED TO THE HOUSE

a mail coach service, which made Repton cling to the amateur view that his theories were his chief claim to distinction. It was also with an eye on the garbled versions of his gardens which he saw growing up round him that he affirms this amateur attitude in no uncertain terms, saying that ". . . it is rather upon my opinions in writing than on the partial and imperfect manner in which my plans have sometimes been executed that I wish my fame to be established."[1]

It was more as a voluminous contributor to the literature of the "paper-battle" than as a fashionable "day-labourer," working, as Jane Austen records, at a rate of five guineas a day,[2] that Repton exerted such an important influence on Regency architecture. The authentic list of his gardens is too vague, and the effect of time and neglect too imponderable, for them to prove a very profitable source of information. It is only if they are considered, as he himself considered them, as experiments from which he derived the principles elaborated in his books, that Repton can be appreciated for what he was; and it is hardly valuing his theories too highly to say that his was the most important individual contribution to the Regency style.

For, as a theorist with a practical knowledge of the medium in which he was working, Repton provides the chief link between the critical outlook on the landscape and the architecture which was evolved to fit in with it. But his published books, compiled as they were from his *Red Book* specifications, show only one aspect of the contribution he made to contemporary architecture; for revealing as they are of the principles on which he worked, their influence, as publications, was probably slight. He himself regretted that the cost of these books made them inaccessible to a public which would be reached by more popular, but probably less worthy, critics of the landscape garden.

It was through his connections with architects and architecture that his influence was more directly felt. Brown had established the precedent for the landscape gardener's inclusion of architecture in his professional repertoire; "having found," as the poet William Mason wrote, in a letter which is quoted by Repton in one of his books, "the great difficulty which must frequently have occurred to him in forming a picturesque whole, where the previous building had been ill placed, or of improper dimensions." For the same Picturesque reasons, Repton also discovered it to be, as he says, "absolutely necessary for the *landscape gardener* to have a competent knowledge of *architecture*."[3] With this in mind the Repton family was turned into a sort of architectural syndicate. Two of his sons were articled to architects. John Adey, who started in the office of Repton's friend, William Wilkins, became a follower of the Gothic style, and, as such, is acknowledged as a collaborator in the *Theory and Practice of Landscape Gardening*. G. S. Repton was one of John Nash's draughtsmen and stayed on in

---

[1] *Theory and Practice of Landscape Gardening* (1802).
[2] "Your best friend on such an occasion," said Miss Bertram calmly, "would be Mr. Repton I imagine. . . . His terms are five guineas a day." *Mansfield Park*.
[3] *Sketches and Hints on Landscape Gardening* (1795).

his office long after an informal partnership between Repton and Nash was dissolved some time about the year 1802. The partnership was a failure from Repton's point of view, but it was one to which Regency architecture was to become enormously indebted when Nash came to project his "garden city" in Regent's Park.

Repton's ultimate victory in the "paper battle" was itself in great measure due to his taking his stand on architectural principles. Ideas as much dependent on mere matters of taste as Price's new-model Picturesque and Payne Knight's vague emulation of landscape painting did not show up particularly well against the eminently architectural quality of the Repton garden. Vivid illustrations of what Repton was up against in the form of gardens interpreting these ideas are found in the early books of John Loudon. The "improvements" illustrated in his *Country Residences* show only too clearly the Picturesque wilderness out of which Repton shepherded the Regency house.

Loudon, who started by setting out to interpret a Price-like picturesqueness in his gardens, and who finished by establishing the so-called "Gardinesque" style of the early Victorians, was later to write enthusiastically of Repton and, in fact, to edit a collected volume of his books; but in *Country Residences* there are no words of comfort for followers of the untouchable Brown. "Trees," he says, "are still planted in clumps and belts; and parks could referred to, laid out in 1804, if possible even more ridiculous in these respects than even Fisherwick, one of Mr. Brown's first efforts. Water is uniformly confined in long canals regularly serpentine; and instances are common, both in England and Scotland, where natural banks and rivers have had their banks shaped, sloped and smoothed, and often their general direction rendered serpentine in imitation of made canals."

Such were the scenes which the painter's hand was to transform into the luxuriant landscapes of the correctly Picturesque. Loudon, contemplating an "upright rock of formal even surface, and naked above," asks himself for example, "in what way would a person, who had never studied drawing, or the principles of painting, attempt to improve that rock?" and comes to the regrettable conclusion that "he would not think of improving it at all." Equipped on the other hand with a knowledge of landscape painting, "inevitably, as if by instinct," he would "disguise its uniformity, either by perpendicular breaks and shadows, or by overhanging it with trees, bushes and creepers." The proper treatment of rocks, which provided such stumbling blocks for the unwary improver, is in fact, one of the chief means towards Loudon's Picturesque effects. With their full accompaniment of overhanging trees, bushes and creepers they are responsible for transforming Barnbarrow from a Brown landscape, whose desolate aspect he emphasises with peculiar relish, to an artistic wilderness to which even the most abject followers of Price could scarcely take exception.

The alternative which Price's school of gardening offered to the selfconscious landscape of Brown was, as Loudon's designs show, one in which the house threatens to go completely to earth. That the garden was the proper place for the cultivation of flowers and the house a suitable subject for architectural design were considerations of little account to those who, like Mr. Gall, "distinguished between the Picturesque and the Beautiful."[1] "Luxuriance" was one of the watchwords of the Picturesque, and the fact that they grew apace sufficient reason for cultivating the ill weeds, often to the detriment of architecture as well as the garden.

For those who, like Loudon, carried the cult of "luxuriance" to its logical conclusions, were in some danger of finding the house tumbling about their ears. Edmund Bartell was one of the most lyrical of the sponsors of undrilled nature as an ornament to the Regency house. "Suffer the tendrils of the ivy," he writes, "to mantle luxuriantly over the windows, opposing its transparent varnished leaves to the too powerful rays of the western sun": but a hint of bitter experience lies behind his suggestion for "a judicious application of the pruning knife" . . . "should it encroach too much (as a favourite frequently does) upon the liberty allowed it."[2] In fact it became a necessary function of such crusaders in the cause of the Picturesque to define limits to the encroachment of plants of this kind which, as Bartell reluctantly admits, are "in great profusion . . . rather injurious in a Picturesque light; giving to a house, or the tower of a church, the appearance of a heavy, uniform bush." Bartell, in common with most of Price's followers, decided on the roof as the limit, although, he says, "they may sometimes be allowed to aspire even to the chimney, where their delicate tendrils flaunting in the breeze are seen to advantage, but if carried further than this the very profusion destroys the effect, and produces a heaviness that is disagreeable."

Profusion of ivy and creepers is admittedly characteristic only of an extreme phase of the Picturesque. Nevertheless they obtained a firm hold on the Regency house. The provision of stone pockets for them at the base of the walls of Panshanger House shows that, in some instances, they even became a "built-in" feature. Panshanger is generally accepted as being a "Repton Garden," and this small feature of it shows an architectural use of his rivals' theories which is typical of Repton's work. There may not have been much room for "luxuriance" in the Repton garden, but its companion "intricacy" ("the due medium between uniformity on the one hand and confusion on the other") was welcomed as a corrective to the barren appearance of Brown's layouts.

The effects of "intricacy" can be appreciated in the Shardeloes (25, 26) improvement, where subsidiary trees are put in to provide what he describes as "variety without fritter" to a landscape which many of his contemporaries would have designed as a series of clumps

[1] Peacock: *Headlong Hall.*
[2] Edmund Bartell, jun.: *Hints for Picturesque Improvements in Ornamental Cottages* (1804).

"like spots of ink, flicked at random out of a pen": as Sir Patrick O'Prism appropriately quoted to Mr. Milestone from Price's *Essay*. The same illustration repays a more careful study as an example of Repton's handling of the landscape: of his thinning of certain tree groups to suggest different planes in the composition, and of the opening up of the surrounding "belt" to suggest an infinite horizon. It is typical of the planting which, under Nash's guidance, was to find its way into the town layout. Even in his formal gardens the demands of "intricacy" were not overlooked. In such cases as the "Chinese" garden proposed for the Brighton Pavilion, a sprinkling of basket flower beds over its lawns is intended to express the requisite balance between the "uniformity" of Brown and the "confusion" of Price (23, 24).

For Repton's part in the "paper battle" was as much one of a mediator as of a participant, and it is perhaps the most important of all his principles that he would not subscribe to any ready-made theory. Repton's was a liberal spirit at a time when most critics of the landscape garden were aspiring to dictatorship. His principles were flexible ones and often turned out to be similar to those which his opponents were putting forward as inexorable laws, a fact which is borne out by his list of parallel statements from *The Analytical Enquiry* and from his own books.

There is a direct connection between Repton's liberalism and the approach to architecture implied in Regency house design. For had he elected to follow either the thorny paths of Price or the broad and comfortable walks to which Payne Knight directed him when he pointed out the "avowed character of art in Italian gardens" as "preferable to the concealed one now in fashion," the landscape garden would in all probability have finished either in the picture-gardening of Downton or in the cultivated wilderness of Foxley. It would certainly never have survived to influence architecture to the extent which it did during the Regency. As it was, Repton's individual example, in surviving the temptations of the Picturesque wilderness, ensured the salvation of the landscape garden as a garden. It also established the broad faith in its principles which is implied in the Regency house. The continuity of this tradition was assured when John Loudon turned from his persecution of Brown and set out to preach the gospel of the "Gardinesque" to the early Victorians.

For the Regency was a time when the faith of landscape gardening badly needed re-statement: a time in which people "looking for a sign" accepted only too readily false prophets like Sir Uvedale Price, and tended to overlook such heralds of Repton's gospel as Henry Holme, Lord Kaimes, who, in his *Elements of Criticism*, had at least taken the preliminary step of making some of his paths straight. His recommendation that "straight walks in recesses do well, they vary the scenery and are favourable to meditation" suggests, for example, a method of approach which became a dogma in the case of Payne Knight's Italian Garden. As a hint it was followed by Repton, who in

30 A Villa at Cheltenham. Characteristic features in windows and balconies combine to give the "cheerfulness, elegance and refinement" emulated by Regency Architects

31, 32 A Convertible Orangery designed by Repton for the Pavilion Grounds: "The Frame and Glass removed in summer it forms a Chiosk"

From "Designs for the Pavilion at Brighton" (1806)

effects largely by scattering suggestive embellishments in an abstract scene. Hence its emphasis on "surprise"; the idea which culminated in the so-called "Chinese" garden described by Sir William Chambers, in which "bats, owls, vultures, and every bird of prey flutter in the groves; wolves, tigers and jackalls howl in the forests; half famished animals wander upon the plains; gibbets, crosses, wheels, and the whole apparatus of torture, are seen from the roads." The architectural features take the form of temples "dedicated to the king of vengeance," while built-in commentaries on these "surprising" scenes are provided in the form of ". . . pillars of stone, with pathetic descriptions of tragical events, and the many horrid acts of cruelty, perpetrated there by outlaws and robbers of former times. . . ."[1] Such flights into the more rarefied regions of the Sublime were certainly found in the Regency garden, but they were hangovers from an orgy of Taste which most of the garden reformers were agreed in condemning. "Surprises" in the Regency garden were more likely to be of an accidental sort, such as the elephant in charge of a groom which Scott encountered in the grounds of Chiswick House.

Payne Knight quotes with disapproval the use of a plaster lion, suitably chained to restrain the terror of his Sublimity, as a garden embellishment, while the lion's head which Cobbett saw spouting water into Mr. Montague's pond in all probability belonged to the same species. Also quoted in the *Principles of Taste* is the *cause célèbre* of Peacock's "Mr. Milestone" . . . "a rock cut into the shape of a giant. In one hand he holds a horn, through which that little fountain is thrown to a prodigious elevation. In the other is a ponderous stone, so exactly balanced as to be apparently ready to fall on the head of any person who may happen to be beneath: and there is Lord Little-brain walking under it."[2] The latter fortunately survived to figure in further pages of Mr. Milestone's improvements; to row on his canal in his "elegant boat," to drive four-in-hand down his belt of limes and to admire the prospect through a telescope from the summit of his garden pavilion; but in Payne Knight's version the rock actually did fall ". . . and, coming nearer to the head of one of the spectators than the laws of the system would allow, it has brought the scheme into such disrepute among the ignorant mechanics and barbarous country gentlemen of the neighbourhood, that there is some danger of the benefit of the example being lost to the public."[3] The example is, however, quoted as being something of an oddity. Nor, apart from a few random examples like the model of Stonehenge at Alton Towers, did the garden ruin long survive the exacting criticism of the garden reformers. The playwright's "clap trap" suggested an analogy according to which such "eye-traps" were condemned as being altogether unworthy of the Picturesque garden, while Repton, with his statement that "sham ruins, sham bridges, and everything which appears what

[1] Sir William Chambers: *Dissertation on Oriental Gardening* (1772).
[2] Peacock: *Headlong Hall* (1806).   [3] Payne Knight: *Analytical Enquiry*.

the case of the Improvement of a cottage at Endsleigh, made just such a terrace "favourable to meditation." Holme above all heralds Repton in his criticism of the landscape garden in general terms at a time when a formidable amount of thought was going into interpreting the letter of its law. The cataloguing of different types of scenery in conformity with the works of "The Painters" is a case in point. Payne Knight defines three types, the *classical* with its associations of "fallen magnificence," the *romantic* ("in which every object is wild, abrupt, and fantastic") and the *pastoral*, which is associated particularly with "neat and comfortable cottages, inhabited by a plain and simple, but not rude or vulgar, peasantry; placed amid cultivated, but not ornamented gardens."

Even more conscientious definitions are given by John Loudon who describes, for example, how *romantic* scenery "unites the grand without the awful, the wild without the savage, the solitary without the forlorn, the cheerful luxuriance and variety of nature, without the teeming abundance and regularity of art."[1] The categories were far from being accepted unconditionally by critics of the landscape garden, but the fact that even Repton subscribed to them in general terms, is sufficient argument for considering them to be widely accepted types. They are, however, less important in themselves than as examples of the consistency between architecture and landscape which was derived from such "associations of ideas." Edmund Bartell, for example, states the view not only of the picture-gardeners but of the common run of Regency architects when he says that ". . . the column, the rich balustrade, and the ruined temple, however beautiful in the pictures of Claude, can find no place but in the elevated scenes to which they belong; so much is due to consistency, and to a proper association of ideas, that if the objects themselves, from which Claude deduced his most beautiful subjects, were placed as the ornaments of a scene in Holland or Flanders, they would be as much out of place, as a Grecian portico attached to a clay-walled cottage."[2]

This accent on the "association of ideas" accounted for many whimsies which appear on the surface of Regency architecture. It has a greater importance in suggesting the idea that the form of the house should reflect something of the form of the garden. Regency architects evolved their individual forms of design largely by way of cultivating an emotional "propriety" between the house and its surroundings. Just what associations of ideas were read into the romantic house in its romantic setting would depend on the extent to which the spectator subscribed to the principles of picture-gardening. But, whatever emotions he may have experienced, they were not likely to be those suggested by the eighteenth-century garden: nor were they likely to be suggested to him in at all the same way.

For the eighteenth-century garden was one which had derived its

---

[1] Loudon: *Country Residences.*
[2] Edmund Bartell, jun.: *Hints for Picturesque Improvements in Ornamental Cottages.*

F

33 Beaumont Street, Oxford

34 St. Mary's College, Mortlake

35 Upper Phillimore Place, London

TRELISSED VERANDAHS

36 With key-pattern Moulding   37 From Cheltenham

38 An Iron Porch from Cheltenham   39 From Tottenham Green East,
                                           London

WINDOWS AND IRONWORK

it is not, disgusts when the truth is discovered" attempted to clear the garden of these characteristic relics of eighteenth-century Taste.[1]

But it was not merely on grounds of intellectual dishonesty that the "eye-trap" was condemned by the arbiters of Regency taste. It was equally because the theatrical convention of treating it as a mere "property": set against the backcloth of an abstract landscape was, in their view, an altogether improper method of suggesting ideas. It was the landscape itself which ought to reflect such "associations." Thus architecture, which had hitherto merely provided a foil to the landscape, became, by way of the principle of "congruity," a part of the landscape itself. ". . . The baronial castle, the ruined abbey, or the humble cottage, by carrying us back to times past, and being combined as objects in a scene," became, in the eyes of such men as Edmund Bartell, "as much a part of nature as the soil itself, the trees, and the grass which adorn it, the horse, the cow, or, in short, any other object animate or inanimate."[1] Hence all the niceties which an age particularly critical of the landscape had distinguished in the natural scene was now to be reflected in the design of the house itself.

The expression of this idea in its most uncompromising terms is found in Loudon's *Country Residences*, in which even individual trees have appropriate emotions ascribed to them. He considers, for example, that "there is a degree of cheerfulness in the light airy forms of the ash, and the bright white of the variegated holly; ease and gracefulness in the festoons of virgin's bower; delicacy in the myrtle, and a peculiar elegance in the sweep of the stem and curve of the branches of the larch." "The oak and chestnut," he adds, "possess forms which have long been associated with grandeur and sublimity."[2]

In conformity with the emotions suggested by the landscape, the house itself adopts an appearance of cheerfulness, melancholy, elegance or sublimity. So much the worse for its inhabitants if the landscape gardener ruled that the surrounding scene was a melancholy one, for then they had to have a melancholy house to match; and Loudon is fully prepared to provide the recipe for designing it. For these victims of the cult of "congruity" he prescribes "a building with few windows, and those also smaller than usual and irregularly placed; this," he adds, as a comfortless precedent, "we sometimes see in old castles, and also in hospitals."[3]

Not every student of the Picturesque would swallow Loudon's prescriptions for doctoring the landscape and its buildings, but there were few who would fail to appreciate that certain types of building were appropriate in certain situations. "An unadorned regular House," for example, would, as Pocock explains, be "suitable for a plain open country, a magnificent Mansion for a country abounding with vegetation, and richly clothed with majestic woods, a modest and retired Cottage is well disposed in a luxurious valley, while in bold and romantic

---

[1] Humphry Repton: *Theory and Practice of Landscape Gardening.*
[2] Loudon: *Country Residences* (1806).   [3] Ibid.: *Rural Residences.*

situations the greatest licence may be given to the imagination whether
in designing a Dwelling in the rural manner of a Cabane Ornée, or
in the picturesque style of a magnificent abbey."[1]

Papworth in his book on *Ornamental Gardening* explains how such
ideas of "congruity" came to affect not only the choice of the site for
a house but the actual style in which it was to be built. Papworth,
among the many and varied talents which make him one of the most
interesting architects of the Regency period, had a literary bent and
subscribed numerous articles to Ackermann's *Forget-me-not Annual*.
Some of these, accompanied by water colour drawings, reproduced
in the best Ackermann tradition, were reprinted in the form of two
books on gardening. They are full of pertinent observations on the
Regency house and garden, which have all the more value coming, as
they do, from an architect who laid out numerous gardens and designed
the houses to go with them. On the subject of "congruity" he elaborates
ideas similar to those put forward by Repton in his *Sketches and Hints
on Landscape Gardening*. If, he says, the site is a plain ". . . embellished
with tall aspiring trees, particularly a mixture of the pine, beech and
fir, with the oak and elm, and the distant scenery composed of long
ranges of lofty hills and the spires of towns and cities, the features of
the architecture should be Grecian, as the prevailing lines of its architecture harmonise both with the broad base on which it stands, and
the spiry forms by which it is surrounded, with all the advantages of
proper opposition without the extremes of contrast, between which
distinction be all that taste requires towards the beauty of its linear
composition. Upon similar principles, if the ground be part of a hill
and the forms of the trees more round, or the structure broken and
romantic, the Gothic of massive or delicate forms may be used; the
former where the effect is rocky, bold and prominent, and the latter
where its parts are polished and refined."[2]

The way in which these ideas were tending to confine the classics
to the plains and relegate the Goths to more Sublime altitudes is further
illustrated by Thompson, who points out that "to construct a Hermitage,
as has sometimes been done, on the road-side of an approach to a
populous town or city, would necessarily be out of true character; it
is in a wild uncultivated country, amidst the picturesque scenery of
crag and precipice, that such objects strike with effect."[3]

Architects were in fact using their lending libraries to some effect
in interpreting the finer points of the Picturesque. From Gilpin and
his like they could even learn which situations were suitable for certain
trees. In describing, for example, the weeping-willow, Gilpin decides
that ". . . we wish it not to skreen the broken buttresses and Gothic
windows of an abbey, nor to overshadow the battlements of a ruined
castle; these offices it resigns to the oak, whose dignity can support

---

[1] W. F. Pocock: *Architectural Designs for Rustic Cottages, Picturesque Dwellings,
Villas Etc.* (1807).
[2] J. B. Papworth: *Ornamental Gardening*.   [3] Thompson: *Retreats* (1835).

them. The weeping willow seeks an humbler scene—some romantic foot-path bridge, which it half conceals—or some glassy pool, over which it hangs its streaming foliage—and dips

> Its pendent boughs, stooping as if to drink. . . .

In the same strain Edmund Bartell, a professed admirer of Gilpin, defines the proper architectural use of creepers. If they are ". . . set to embower the trellis work," . . . "plant," he directs, "the monthly rose, and clymatis or virgin bower, which grow luxuriantly, and when in blossom have a beautiful and rich appearance; but no common creepers or honeysuckles should be seen near the *Cottage Ornée*: their province is to shade and enrich the peasant's cot."

That the consideration of planting in these terms materially contributed to Regency architecture is shown in the house in Brockwell Park, Brixton, designed by Papworth, presumably for the owner of the estate, the glassmaker, John Blades. The landscaped stream of the river Effra reflects a use of the weeping-willow such as Gilpin must assuredly have approved of, while the house itself (although it may be considered to be ripe for a "judicious application" of Edmund Bartell's pruning knife) presents a well-preserved picture of the effects at which Regency architects were aiming in the use of climbing plants.

In this and in other ways planting enormously affected the Regency house. For not only were different styles of building considered appropriate in different types of landscape, but the actual design of the house, its silhouette and the grouping of its parts, was carefully studied in relation to the scenic background. Thus, "when there is a varied outline of hills, or trees to form the background," Atkinson decides that ". . . a straight or square roof is not much to be objected to";[1] the inference of course being that, with a less "varied outline," it was. Materials too, came in for some consideration in relation to the scenery, and Edmund Bartell joins issue with Sir Uvedale Price on the question of roofing cottages with thatch. Price, on the grounds that thatch in time acquired "something of a damp dirty look," which was increased "both in reality and appearance" by the effect of trees or plants climbing over it, suggested the equally Picturesque alternative of covering the roof with a hard material which "may without injury be half concealed by either of them"; . . . "It rarely happen," he adds, "that there is any thing in the look of a covering that could make one regret its partial concealment."[2] Bartell, on the other hand, seems to have considered the correct association of ideas to be of greater moment than either the appearance or the reality of damp and dirt, and sticks to his point that thatch is "indispensable" in rural buildings.

Such ideas as these made material contributions to the design of the Regency house. It was with one eye on the landscape garden and the

[1] William Atkinson: *Picturesque Views of Cottages* (1805).
[2] Sir Uvedale Price: *Essays on the Picturesque*.

other on what Godwin describes as "a piquant assemblage of parts" in their buildings that the Regency arrived at its individual style of building. In fact criticism of Brown's gardens was probably caused less by dissatisfaction with the gardens themselves than by their being considered unsuitable for the symmetrical houses which went with them. As it was put by Loudon, ". . . the chief defect which has all along attended the progress of architecture in this country is the neglect of harmonising the buildings with the situation."[1] Architects had stood still while the landscape gardeners had gone off to explore the Picturesque. They had hitherto made no attempt to reconcile the house with the compositions cultivated in the garden. Thus Payne Knight, contemplating the "poor square edifice exposed alone . . . amidst spacious lawns intersperced with irregular clumps, or masses of wood, and sheets of water," decides that he does not know "a more melancholy object: it neither associates nor harmonises with any thing; and as the beauties of symmetry, which might appear in its regularity, are only perceived when that regularity is seen; that is, when the building is shown from a point of sight at right angles with one of the fronts, the 'Man of Taste' takes care that it never shall be so shown; but that every view of it shall be oblique, from the tangent of a curve in a serpentine walk; from whence it appears neither quite regular, nor quite irregular; but with that sort of lame and defective uniformity, which we see in an animal that has lost a limb."[2]

The alternative remedies for this lack of "congruity" between house and garden were those of altering the garden to suit the house or of altering the house to suit the garden. Both of these alternatives were appreciated by Regency architects, but in an age in which such definite ideas on the landscape were abroad, there could be little doubt as to which would prove the most popular course. It was in fact one of the most important considerations in Regency architecture that it tried to adapt the house to the form of the Picturesque landscape. Although the Picturesque in this context became an essentially practical issue, it is still difficult to disentangle it from its literary associations; if only because it is so closely bound up with the revival of the Gothic style, which offered special opportunities for irregular grouping. There must have been many an architect who professed a proper sensibility to the emotions associated with Gothic architecture merely as an excuse for designing an irregular house.

Such was probably the case with James Malton who, in his book of *Designs for Villas* gives, among a series of extravagant Gothic designs, an illustration of the situation considered appropriate for an irregular "castellated" house. It is shown first on a level site, for which any architect with a feeling of "congruity" would have preferred a design in the "Grecian" style, and afterwards on a romantic wooded site where its solitary tower shows to advantage when viewed from any angle. Compositions of this sort gave an effective answer to Payne Knight's

[1] Loudon: *Country Residences.*   [2] Payne Knight: *Analytical Enquiry.*

40   An Aviary for a Flower Garden

41   A Garden Seat

42 A Garden Seat

From Ackermann's "Repository of Arts, Literature and Fashion"

GARDEN ORNAMENTS BY J. B. PAPWORTH

43   The Earl of Shrewsbury's Garden at Alton Towers, Staffordshire

44   The Cloister, Ashridge, Hertfordshire. *James Wyatt, Architect*

criticism that the house ought to look well from any point in the landscape garden.

But, while the Gothic was accepted as the proper medium in which to design the Picturesque house, there are rare cases of architects working out their own salvation without resorting to the ready-made recipe it provided. Nash, for example, experimented along these lines in an indeterminate Italian style at Cronkhill. Perhaps the most individual of all attempts in this direction are the designs made by Joseph Gandy under the title of *Designs for Cottages and Rural Buildings* (1805) and *The Rural Architect* (1805). In these books Gandy emerges from his place in the shadows of Soane's drawing office and proves himself to be at least a paper architect of no mean ability. The problem he sets himself to solve is the same one that was occupying the Gothic Revivalists. It is stated in his introduction in terms as free from the usual jargon of architects trading in the Picturesque as the designs which follow are free of the mannerisms of their architecture. He puts his case in the form of ". . . a question submitted to the Public, whether Architectural Designs, in general should be uniform, that is, having corresponding fronts on each side of a centre, or whether they should be composed of parts dissimilar, though harmonious."[1]

Gandy, in fact, was doing just what Payne Knight was doing. He was examining the regular Palladian house from different standpoints in the landscape garden and deciding, like him, that what he saw was a failure from the architectural point of view. All of the designs revolve round the consideration that, as he puts it, "uniform buildings have but one point of view from whence their parts are corresponding; from every other point they fall into the Picturesque by the change of perspective." Gandy's buildings are accordingly designed to "fall into the Picturesque" from such varied points of view as might be given of them from the "natural" garden. At the same time they make the most of the surroundings as seen from the house.

For the symmetrical house not only ignored the oblique viewpoints from the landscape garden. It took scarcely more account of the view of the garden from the house. Gandy's type of Picturesque house was equally designed to answer Knight's criticism that the symmetrical house was out of character with the landscape garden and the one that ". . . The view from one of these solitary mansions is still more dismal than that towards it."[2] The irregular placing of windows in positions from which they could command the best prospects was one remedy for this which was widely used in the Regency house. Another consisted of altering the shape of the windows themselves. Gandy experimented with horizontal types which could command a wide range of scenery. Other architects multiplied the number of lights in their windows and bent them into the bays and bows which became a characteristic of the Regency house. Alternatively, as Repton recommended in his

[1] J. M. Gandy: *Designs for Cottages, Cottage Farms and other Rural Buildings* (1805).
[2] *Analytical Enquiry.*

"improvements" at Barmingham Hall, they made use of the tall Tudor window or similar forms of Gothic bay.

Another way in which "congruity" with the romantic landscape was suggesting experiments in "Picturesque," or, as architects would say to-day "asymmetrical," compositions was in encouraging architects to look at their designs as a whole and not, as they had previously tended to do, as a building set about with a series of incongruous "appendages." For it was a tendency, which on the whole seems to have been identifiable with Brown and his imitators, to build the "offices" of a house in a separate wing and to surround it with a screen of shrubbery, with the idea of hiding everything except the symmetrical block of the main building. The result, as Payne Knight describes it, was that the "wretched square solitary mansion-house" was left "to exhibit its pert bald front between the dwarf shrubberies, which seem like whiskers added to the portico or entrance."[1] That even an architect so well versed in the intricacies of the Picturesque as J. B. Papworth was not above designing in this way is shown in the Brockwell Park house, in which the planting on one side masks a series of stable buildings. It does, however, attempt a remedy, suggested by Payne Knight, of using planting to break up what he calls the "subordinate ranges of less elevated building," so that "though the forms had individually been bad, yet by dividing and grouping them with trees, pleasing effects of composition might have been produced; at once to gratify the eye with some varieties of tint and light and shadow, and to amuse the imagination with some appearance of intricacy."

It was largely under the guidance of the Reptons that the more adventurous spirits among Regency architects made a clean break with this practice and with all similar compromises such as the expedient of hiding the offices behind mounds. "Mr. Repton," as Papworth describes this important departure from the symmetrical house, ". . . soon combined the offices with the plantations, and brought them from their accustomed seclusion into view, because of their usefulness in increasing the richness of the composition, and to lead to and support the chief building, by giving it accompaniments of its own kind and character."[2]

Here again the Gothic style offered a ready-made precedent, which was used, as such, by architects like John Randall, who includes a design for a small Gothic house in his *Villa Residences*. His drawing shows an almost regular house with a kitchen attached: a plan in fact which is not far removed from the one Papworth used in the Brockwell Park house. Had the design been "Grecian," the kitchen wing would have had to be concealed behind a shrubbery so that the symmetrical effect of the front should not be destroyed; but, being Gothic, it can be made to "lead to and support the chief building." The shaping of the "Eating Parlour" so that it commands a variety of prospects completes the departure from the symmetrical plan. It also rounds off

[1] Payne Knight: *Analytical Enquiry*.   [2] J. B. Papworth: *Ornamental Gardening*.

a house which can take its place happily in an irregular landscape while itself enjoying varied views of its surroundings. It might be imagined that this alone would provide a sufficient justification for the irregular house, but it was characteristic of the Regency to produce utilitarian arguments in support of its aesthetic ideas, and the Picturesque plan did not escape consideration in this more prosaic light. Arguments of this sort are produced by Thompson, who explains how, in designing small houses, "it is desirable to group together their little appendages, not only because they require less of walling, and are therefore less expensive, but because the combination is calculated to give consequence to a habitation that would otherwise appear insignificant."[1] It was also put forward as a consideration which was likely to weigh more with the new-rich client for a battlemented villa than any amount of aesthetic arguments would have done, that irregular buildings ". . . also convey the appearance of greater magnitude than they actually possess, by the successive disclosure of their features to the view."[2]

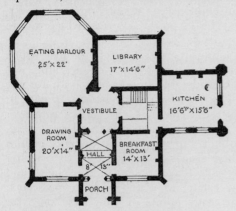

PLAN OF A SMALL GOTHIC HOUSE
From John Randall's *Villa Residences*.

The same tendency to make Picturesque capital out of incidents which in the eighteenth-century garden would have been ignored, if not deliberately kept out of sight, came to affect very much more than the "little appendages" of the house. Ample illustrations of this are provided in the pattern books illustrating "Rural Improvements," by means of which architects hoped to get the custom of the new-rich settlers in the countryside. Dairies, stables, cottages, chicken houses, dog kennels; all are considered as potential contributors to the completed picture of the estate, while there is a consistent hankering after the idea of the so-called *Ferme Ornée*. The latter was, however, a form of landscaping which the Regency generally stopped short of. The Cobbett tradition represented too solid a buffer against its being carried out. For it was one thing for the "cit" to make a fool of himself in his own grounds. It was quite another when he tried to involve the serious business of agriculture in his capers, and Repton did well for the relations between landlord and tenant when he advised the "improver" to stop at the confines of the gentleman's park. Cows could perhaps be used as a substitute for deer in ornamenting the scenery of the park, but the neighbouring farmland was better left alone. For one thing the flowers with which Addison had advised his readers to embellish their hedgerows were only too likely to be the farmer's most noxious

[1] Thompson: *Retreats* (1835).   [2] Ibid.

G

weeds. Perhaps the most conciliatory gesture made by any of the Regency improvers towards a suspicious agricultural community was the one made by the Earl of Shrewsbury when he used stucco sheep to "enliven" the scenery of Alton Towers.

But while the enthusiast for the Picturesque was looking wistfully at the material which Repton was conspiring with rural politics to deprive him of, it was not beyond the improver's ingenuity to find substitutes for it nearer home. Of this nature was the "improvement" which John Plaw proposed to his client, Colonel Thornton: ". . . I suggested," he says, "an idea to the Colonel to form an encampment of his spaniels and pointers on an eminence, in a stately grove of oaks, accompanied occasionally by his Hawks and Falconers, which would have had a very Picturesque effect in the park."[1]

This question of where the Picturesque was to stop: of just which incidents in the landscape, if any, were to be left out of its frame, was one which turned out to be of considerable importance both for the garden and for the architecture which was so closely bound up with it. For when, in his quest for Picturesque material, the garden improver ultimately came to the boundary of his estate and was faced, as it were, with the spectacle of William Cobbett hurling yeoman defiance at him from the other side, the time had clearly come for him, to consider his relationship to the outside world. The problem of the "belt" and of defining the boundary of the estate, to which Repton gave such careful consideration, were from many points of view vital ones for Regency architects. Not the least important aspect of them is that they made the improver consider "congruity" in its broader sense, in terms of man's relation to the scenes he was making. The result of this inquiry was the discovery that the humanist ideals which had animated the earlier landscape garden were largely incompatible with the aims of the Regency improvers.

For the eighteenth-century garden had not been designed for man as he was, but for the poetic figures who featured in the pictures of Claude and the Poussins. The garden was first made in the image of "The Painters," after which contemporary man fitted himself into the frame as best he could. Given these conditions it did not take long to discover that in the garden in which every prospect pleased it was only man who was vile. He was really only tolerable in the humanist landscape at all if he were likewise in a complete "state of nature." Lady Suffolk's letters suggest that attempts were even made to live up to this idea.

This aspect of the landscape garden was one which, when they weighed it in their eminently practical balances, the Regency gardeners found to be particularly wanting. A scheme which failed to take account of all the incidents in the landscape, from the "little appendages" of the house to the Colonel's spaniels, was one for which they could find very little use. What the Regency asked of the garden was that it

[1] John Plaw: *Ferme Ornée or Rural Improvements* (1800).

45 The Apotheosis of the Tent. The Steyne Front of the Pavilion (1815–20)

From "The Royal Pavilion at Brighton," by John Nash (1824)

46   An "Umbrella" of Copper on an Iron Framework

47   A Seat with a Tent Covering

From Papworth's "Rural Residences" (1818)

DESIGNS FOR GARDEN SEATS

should provide a setting for themselves, for their own particular possessions and eccentricities: not one for St. Ursula's virgins or the
herds of Battus. Under Repton the Regency gardeners learnt how to
take the humanism underlying the eighteenth-century garden and
adopt it to this broader and more practical view of humanity. Hence
their emphasis on homely details, such as the smoke rising from the
cottage chimney, which Repton made a feature in his landscape at
Blaise Castle. It was an idea which was carried a stage further by Nash
when he used the argument that the bargees would "enliven" the scene
as an excuse for carrying the canal across Regent's Park, in full view
of the houses which overlooked it.

In this idea of the "landscape for living in" the cult of "congruity"
was carried to its logical conclusions and, on the way, it produced one
of the essential principles of Regency architecture. This principle was
summarised by John Plaw when he wrote that "in the habitations of
man it is necessary to combine the *utile* with the *dulce*."[1] As might
be expected there were many and conflicting ideas on the way in which
the desired union was to be brought about. That some consideration
should be given to the Picturesque in a practical light was, however,
an idea which was generally accepted by Regency architects. It remained
one of the saving graces of an architecture which, as Loudon's "improvements" show, threatened to be altogether submerged by the rising tide
of sensibility to the Picturesque. The principle of utility was invoked,
like many others, on both sides in the "paper battle," but it was Repton
in particular who used it to define his attitude to garden design. "I
am," he says, "not less an admirer of those scenes which painting
represents; and I have discovered that *utility* must often take the lead
of beauty, and *convenience* be preferred to Picturesque effect, in the
neighbourhood of man's habitation."[2]

The zeal with which architects pursued the principles of *utility* and
convenience increased throughout the Regency period, and at its close,
William Godwin is found justifying the immense towers of his houses
in Ireland on such various grounds as that they provided a means of
"telegraphic communication" with adjoining estates or that they "afford
an opportunity to the ladies of the family to accompany the sportsmen
in the chase, with their eyes, if not more amazonially on horseback."[3]
The tower may fairly be considered as being the last stronghold of
the Picturesque to fall before the onslaught of "utility." Mr. Ward
when he started to build a tower in his garden at Westerham, some
thirty miles from London, needed no better excuse than that it might
give him a glimpse of St. Paul's; but, short of such "Follies," Regency
architects put forward some practical justification for most of their
excursions into the Sublime and the Picturesque.

When, for example, John Plaw takes it into his head to design a

---

[1] John Plaw: *Sketches for Country Houses, Villas and Rural Dwellings* (1800).
[2] Humphry Repton: *Sketches and Hints on Landscape Gardening.*
[3] Francis Goodwin: *Rural Architecture.*

circular cottage ("For a Fisherman or Herdsman") he goes so far as to justify his whimsy by explaining that it is "calculated to give the least resistance to the wind."[1] Similarly when he indulges his fancy for the Picturesque in designing what he describes as a "wood pile house," the inside of which is "stuck with moss" and the walls made of oak boughs bedded in clay and straw, this purely Picturesque object is fitted out as a "convenience" in the most Municipal sense of the word and its "utility" justified by saying that such a feature is called for "in a park or plantation where the walks or rides are extensive."[2] In "preserving the *equivoque* under the character and appearance of a wood pile" John Plaw may seem to have gone unnecessarily far out of his way to produce the requisite union between the *utile* and the *dulce*. His excursions in this direction were, however, paralleled by other and more significant attempts to bring the Picturesque into line with architectural principles.

Robert Lugar, in his *Architectural Sketches for Cottages, Rural Dwellings and Villas*, subscribes, for example, to the view that "The Architect, not less than the painter, should feel the true value of varied lines in the contour of buildings, and he should frequently compose with the painter's eye. The broken line must be considered peculiarly in character for a Picturesque Cottage, whether it be the habitation of a gentleman or a peasant . . ." but at the same time a proper attention to "utility" suggests the architectural quality which, even in the wildest flights of Picturesque fancy, the Regency seldom lost sight of. The same "varied and broken line" should, he says, "arise from apparent wants; from the necessity of the case," and not for the sake of merely destroying a continued line. . . . "A lean-to closet, a bow-window, a pent-house, chimneys carried high and in masses, or gable-ends," are suggested as "suitable Picturesque objects," which "will generally produce the wished-for effect."

That "utility" and "convenience" could even, on occasions, prove themselves of some practical value is shown by Lugar's suggestion that "cleanliness and dryness, in opposition to neglect and ruin," are ". . . objects of more real satisfaction than can be afforded by moss-grown houses and mutilated walls. Nor can I suppose that, in adhering to these attentions to comfort, the Picturesque will be at all in danger."[3] Considered in such terms they were at least a better insurance against a rheumatic old age than the same architect's design for a "Cottage in Ruins" (11), in reference to which he explains that ". . . the idea to be conveyed was an abbey mutilated, and to show the cottage as if dressed out of the remains." The argument might have been even more salutary had it not been such an adaptable one. For it was no less possible to interpret it as William Atkinson did, when he said that in

[1] John Plaw: *Sketches for Country Houses, Villas and Rural Dwellings*.
[2] Ibid.: *Ferme Ornée or Rural Improvements* (1800).
[3] *Architectural Sketches for Cottages, Rural Dwellings and Villas, in the Grecian, Gothic and Fancy Styles* (1805).

a house built of black Whinstone stone, moss and lichens on the walls served a useful purpose because they helped to keep out the cold.[1]

But however doubtful its practical value may have been, the cult of "utility" vastly altered the appearance of the Regency garden. For such "unmeaning excrescences" as Payne Knight considered garden temples to be, there was little room in the "functional" Regency garden. Repton, when he proposed to convert an existing building at Blaise Castle into an ornament of this sort, might justify it on the grounds that it was destined to be frequented by the owner's mother and could thus be considered as a "temple dedicated to filial piety" of a utilitarian variety, but less limited substitutes than this had to be found for the "eye-traps" of the eighteenth-century garden, and the argument of "utility" was often strained to breaking point in supplying them. The search for the garden ornament was, however, somewhat helped by the new moral tone. which was creeping into garden design. Distinction between sensibility and sentimentality had never been the strong point of a form of design which had littered the eighteenth-century garden with inscriptions on any suitably elevated subject, and in many aspects of the Regency garden sentimentality definitely got the upper hand. Shenstone's inscriptions at the Leasowes had been recommended by an earlier critic of the Brown Garden, the Reverend Craddock, in his *Village Memoirs*, as a suitable feature for the improved Picturesque garden, and the idea could not fail to appeal to the literary element among Regency architects. But to accept the idea of the inscription was one thing: it was quite another to approve of Shenstone's particular form of poetic symbolism. Like so many features of the eighteenth-century garden it savoured too much of an irrelevant humanism to meet with the Regency Improver's approval, and the general tendency was rather to find subjects for inscriptions in those homely incidents which suggested so many features of the Regency garden. The result took the form of such fine flowers of sentimentality as the method proposed by John Plaw for ". . . commemorating some favourite animal for past services." "The skull of a horse," he suggests, "may be placed over a mural tablet, where may be recorded the feats of that noble animal, and the water-trough may represent the sarcophagus."[2] Similarly Edmund Bartell decides that he would not ". . . hesitate to affix an inscription . . . in some instances, even to the cottage itself, . . . provided there were any particular circumstances in the scenery etc., to call it forth," and enumerates, "among such circumstances" . . . "the retrospect of past events, the death of a friend, the uncertainties of life, and the pleasures of rural retirement."[3]

In the obituary inscription and its companion "The Cenotaph" Regency gardeners found some substitute for the more grandiloquent melancholy of the eighteenth-century ruin. Constable's picture of "The Cenotaph" is a memorial to this aspect of Regency Taste and, at

[1] William Atkinson: *Picturesque Views of Cottage* (1805).
[2] John Plaw: *Ferme Ornée, or Rural Improvements* (1800).
[3] Edmund Bartell, jun.: *Hints for Picturesque Improvements in Ornamental Cottages*.

the same time, a not inappropriate reminder that Landseer is just around the corner. For Landseer's idea that nature had moral lessons to teach was one which was already far advanced in the Regency garden. The extent to which it had become built-in to garden embellishments can be seen in Papworth's book on *Ornamental Gardening*. In it he includes a design for an apiary, explaining, in support of the idea, that ". . . few studies afford more satisfactory resorts to persons of leisure and reflection than are to be obtained by contemplating the habits and conduct of these little animals, from which the lessons of prudence, industry and social virtue, may be correctly acquired, as from the deep-studied instruction of the schools."

Where Papworth sends "persons of leisure" to the bee for moral instruction, Robertson finds a more frankly "natural" reason for sending young ladies to the aviary. In his *Designs in Architecture*, a rustic aviary is recommended as a suitable source of instruction for them, since ". . .the numerous little wants that are to be supplied, and provision made for, from the nesting time to the fledging of the young birds, afford such pleasures as must endear it to them." The aviary is a favourite feature of the Regency garden and Robertson must be numbered among its most eloquent sponsors. The rush of sensibility to the aviary could not, in fact, be described in more vivid terms than those in which he suggests designing a kind of composite Aviary Conservatory and Music Room. In support of the idea he explains how ". . . the pleasing transition from the employment of one of our most refined senses, in contemplating the beautiful and delicate products of nature, to the gratification of another, (not less refined) by a delightful harmony, formed from the union of the notes of art, and those of 'nature's choristers,' must cause such agreeable sensations, as can be known to those only who have experienced it."[1]

Such reminders of Nature's moral lessons were helping considerably to remedy that "unfurnished" appearance of the Regency garden which had started Papworth on his search for suitable embellishments for it. Meanwhile, architects were deriving fresh inspiration by way of the cultivation of nature's "agreeable sensations" at first hand. "Taste, accompanying Rural Simplicity" is the title of the allegorical frontispiece with which John Plaw introduces his *Rural Architecture*, and this elevating union was to be responsible for a numerous progeny of embellishments in the "Rustic" style. For the Regency garden reformer, in averting his eyes from the spectacle of Lady Suffolk's "back to nature" movement, tended to find himself literally looking at the roots of landscape design. As a result he was himself soon sponsoring an uncompromising naturalistic movement: a movement in which garden ornaments were made of roots, moss, bark and turf: the essential "materials of nature."

It was not a movement which was altogether approved of by the pundits of correct Taste. Payne Knight condemns its products along

[1] W. Robertson: *Designs in Architecture* (1800).

48, 49   The "Modern Living Room" contrasted with the "Ancient Cedar Parlour"

From Repton's "Fragments of the Theory and Practice of Landscape Gardening" (1816)

50　Regency Ironwork is seen at its best and most imaginative in
Cheltenham: Balconies in Priory Parade

with the garden temple as having "a still stronger character of affecta-
tion" than the latter, and flogs the old horse of "utility" to produce
an argument that ". . . to adapt the genuine style of a herdsman's hut,
or a ploughman's cottage, to the dwellings of opulence and luxury,
is as utterly impossible, as it is to adapt their language, dress, and manners
to the refined usages of polished society."[1] All the same these features
contributed generously to many Regency gardens, as is shown by
Loudon's description of that dump for most of the questionable by-
products of the Picturesque, the Earl of Shrewsbury's garden at Alton
Towers. The Earl, who seems to have indulged in a sort of stylistic
kleptomania, concentrated his most striking acquisitions in a valley
extending below the house. Loudon, who describes its appearance when
he visited Alton Towers (43) during the hey-day of the Earl's "improvements," in 1828, describes this valley as ". . . displaying such a labyrinth
of terraces, curious architectural walls, trellis-work, arbours, vases,
statues, stone stairs, wooden stairs, turf stairs, pavements, gravel and
grass walks, ornamental buildings, bridges, porticos, temples, pagodas,
gates, iron railings, parterres, jets, ponds, streams, seats, fountains,
caves, flower-baskets, waterfalls, rocks, cottages, trees, shrubs, beds of
flowers, ivied walls, rockwork, shell work, root work, moss houses,
old trunks of trees, entire dead trees etc., that it is utterly impossible
for words to give any idea of the effect."[2]

When words failed the loquacious Loudon the occasion must indeed
have been a remarkable one, and even the present remains of Alton
Towers are a remarkable memorial to the man who is commemorated
in a temple housing his statue as having ". . . made the desert smile."
Papworth, who himself contributed to the embellishment of Alton
Towers, had defined the gardener's aim as being one of "filling the
mind with varied incident and contrasting subject," and whatever else
it did, Alton Towers at least achieved this effect. Against this tendency
to architectural constipation in the Regency garden, the "rage for
utility" acted as a healthy corrective. Once more it was Repton who,
through a proper regard for "congruity" and "convenience," shepherded the main flock of Improvers as clear of the Earl's smiling desert
as he did of Price's less aimiable wilderness.

The mature Repton garden certainly had its embellishments, just as
it had its Picturesque intricacies, but they are set in the solid frame of
his "principles"; they never become the subject matter of the picture
itself. Repton, in his handling of the Picturesque, seldom descended, as so
many of his contemporaries did, to "genre" painting. A good illustration
of his mature style, in which ornaments play an important part, is the
design of that "child of my age and declining years," as Repton called
it, the project for the Ashridge garden. The child of his age it may
have been: the design was none the less engendered in earlier years
when, in defining the cause for which he was fighting in the "paper
battle," he wrote that he did not profess to follow either Le Nôtre or

[1] Payne Knight: *Analytical Enquiry*.   [2] *Encyclopedia of Gardening* (1850).

Brown, but, ". . . selecting beauties from the style of each, to adopt so much of the grandeur of the former as may accord with a palace, and so much of the grace of the latter as may call forth the charms of natural landscape."[1]

It was by following this middle path that Repton, almost alone among the Regency improvers, managed to reach a practical objective: in other words, that he managed to make a garden. It is just this fact that it is a garden and not a landscape or a picture which is the essential point of the Ashridge design. In its parterres, rock garden, *cabinet de verdure*, and *rosarium* it makes use of features which had been as rigidly excluded by Brown as they had been, many of them, over-elaborated by Le Notre. The particular weakness of the "Picturesque" garden was not, as so many of its critics like to think, that it was not sufficiently Picturesque. Its weakness was that it was not sufficiently much of a garden. Those who followed its "verdurous glooms and winding mossy ways" found, as Keats did, that they couldn't see what flowers were at their feet. As a matter of fact there were seldom any there. Repton pointed out that a garden is one thing and a landscape another. His *Fragment* explaining a plan "To a Lady who confessed she did not understand either a Plan or a Map" was chosen as a suitable occasion for springing this distinction on a public from which he foresaw some criticism of the formal lawns, rose beds and *berceaux* which he had come to consider appropriate in the flower garden. "I am aware," he says, "that this will cause some alarm to those who fancy all NATURE at variance with ART, and who will exclaim, that this is going back to the old fashioned formal gardening of former days; I answer, by reminding them, that I am not now describing a landscape, but a garden; and A GARDEN IS A WORK OF ART, USING THE MATERIALS OF NATURE."[2] It was a simple enough definition, but one which might profitably have been made more often, in view of the exclusion of so many of nature's materials from the Regency garden. Such a declaration, coming, for example, from Payne Knight, would have been of more practical value than his tortuous argument that if it was permissible to train trees into the shape of dogs it was no less so to train dogs into the shape of trees.

But although Repton's later designs turned again to flower gardens and formality, they seldom excluded the landscape. In the case of Ashridge the formal features were actually woven into the landscape composition. Ideas on planting were, however, adapting themselves to the growing interest in horticulture which is epitomised in the foundation of the "Horticultural Society" in 1812. The Arboretum at Ashridge is a typical result of this. In another direction, Taste was symbolically reconciled with a more practical view of the landscape when Beckford consulted Cobbett on the planting of his American trees at Fonthill. But although trees were tending to become the "specimens" of the Victorian garden, their main function was still to define the foreground,

---

[1] H. Repton: *The Theory and Practice of Landscape Gardening* (1803).
[2] *Fragments on the Theory and Practice of Landscape Gardening* (1816).

background and middle distance of the landscape. To maintain a proper balance between horticulture, as such, and landscape layout became an important consideration in garden layout, and, like so many features of the Regency garden, it had a considerable affect on architecture. For it suggested a new relationship between the house and garden: one in which a studied formality round the house itself led to a park planted in conformity with landscape principles. It was a type of garden which had already been suggested by Lord Kames when he urged the gardener "to lead the mind insensibly from regularity to a bold variety."[1]

The terracing which Francis Goodrich laid out round the house when he carried out his alterations at Prior Park shows how this idea was adopted by Regency architects. By means of the terrace the eye is led into a landscape which before had come right up to the walls of the house. The conservatory too contributes to this effect. Its character of defining an intermediate stage between house and garden was sufficiently appreciated by architects bent on leading the mind ". . . insensibly from regularity to a bold variety." Papworth, for example, records how this consideration had "drawn the conservatory from its heretofore distant station and connected it with the dwelling, ultimately blending it with the garden, while its lawns and walks, no longer separate and distinct, certainly afforded by this juncture a large portion of healthful and pleasurable occupation."[2] The great curving conservatory at Sezincote (80), which links the main living-rooms with the garden on two separate levels, is perhaps one of the best remaining examples of this "ultimate blending" of house and garden by way of the conservatory.

The conservatory provided one means of linking the house with the garden. A more direct one was provided by that characteristic Regency innovation, the french window. It was a feature which not only answered the demand for making the landscape a scene for living in rather than a prospect framed in a drawing-room window: it also made practical other characteristic additions to the house, in the form of balconies and verandahs. The value of verandahs themselves in breaking down the barrier between house and garden is appreciated by Francis Goodwin in describing his use of them at Lissadell House, in Ireland. "The verandah," he says, "may be said to take the room itself abroad, for when rendered so attractive as it may be here, it would frequently seduce the work-table or the reading-table into its own neutral ground, between the house and the open air."[3]

The use of verandahs and french windows necessarily affected the planning of the house, and Papworth ascribes to them the tendency to do away with the basement storey and place the living-rooms on the garden level. "The chief apartments," he says "are now therefore placed on the level of the ground, and have free access to the lawn or terrace by casements that descend to the very floor. This has been attended by the introduction of colonnades and verandahs that throw

---

[1] *Elements of Criticism.*   [2] *Ornamental Gardening* (1823).
[3] Francis Goodwin: *Rural Architecture.*

H

agreeable shade on the apartments, and which become new ones for occasional reading or study."[1]

By way of using these features, Regency architects were learning to think of the garden in terms of the house, as an outdoor living space closely connected with the indoor rooms. In such terms Papworth defines the lawn, as being a "substitute for the broad gravel, or stone terraces that were formerly adopted; it now receives the inhabitants from the windows of the apartments, and, in fact, the lawn has become a favourite auxiliary to every apartment of the house."[2]

It must not, however, be imagined that the common run of Regency architects considered these new features in such a practical light. It was Papworth's business as a critic of the garden to sort out the wood from the trees. Most practising architects were content with the mere picturesqueness of the wood, and the french window and the verandah tended to be used less on their practical merits than because they fitted in conveniently with a romantic view of architecture. The suggested "improvement" to the house which Mr. Hooker built on to the gatehouse of Tonbridge Castle provides a working example of this. It shows how a practical "improvement," in the form of a house better adapted to its garden, was only incidental to an improvement of its literary qualities. For although Mr. Hooker showed a proper feeling for the associations of the Gothic ruins in building such a house at all, yet the result is one which, as Mr. Milestone would have said, had "never been touched by the finger of taste." Above all there is lamentable lack of "congruity" between the style of the house and that of the existing ruin. The first step has therefore been to add a Gothic touch to the windows. Then comes the shaping of the house and its surroundings according to Picturesque principles, and, on the way, the clearing of the shrubbery. The way to the garden is now clear, and a range of french windows opens the way to the "healthful and pleasurable occupation" of cultivating a flower garden.

It is not difficult to appreciate how a more architectural treatment of the garden followed on improvements of this sort: how people who could now step so easily from the house to the garden came to consider the design of intermediate stages. The bringing of the conservatory "from its heretofore distant situation" so that it acted as a garden room opening off the house was the prelude to a widespread use of covered walks and terraces linking up with the house. Repton chooses a house whose main living-rooms are enfiladed with a 300-feet-long range of conservatories and plant houses to explain his plan ". . . to a lady who confessed that she did not understand a plan or a map": and in the same design he makes a free use of trellised arcades for climbing plants.

It was through the conservatory that Regency architects found the way to the flower garden, and it was in this "casket in which are to be found the jewels of the vegetable creation" that they discovered the material for linking house and garden together. For it was not only

---

[1] *Ornamental Gardening.* [2] Ibid.

51, 52 Terraces in the Stone Vernacular at Cheltenham. Lansdowne Terrace (52) was designed by J. B. Papworth (*c.* 1825)

53   At Guildford, Surrey

54   In Pentonville Road, London

55   A Clumsy Essay in Greco-
Egyptian at Stamford

56   A Porch in the Paragon, Clifton

DOOR DESIGNS

flowers of speech that were cultivated in the conservatory. It also produced climbing plants which could be trained over verandahs and porches: even over the house itself. The "trillis," as Pocock calls it, "to support the shooting tendrils of the vine and gay luxuriance of the passion flower"[1] provided another serviceable means of bringing the house and garden together.

To get as close as they could to nature was, in one sense or another, the consistent ambition of Regency architects. They had started by carrying the house into the landscape. They finished by bringing the garden into the house. Such designs as Papworth's for a lakeside cottage show the final stages in this manœuvre. It is entered by a rustic porch, "supported by the stems of elm trees," the hall and staircase are decorated with trellising, made of wicker basketwork, flower stands and brackets decorate the staircase whose handrails are also of basketwork; and over all grow flowers. ". . . The walls everywhere are adorned by them, and some are trained over the trellis of the ceilings, whence they hang in festoons and unite their branches."[2]

Such designs as this represent a reconciliation between "Art" and "Nature" which was of infinitely more architectural value than the one which emulated "Rural Simplicity" in a moss house. In the flowered verandah and the trellised balustrade art showed both a more seemly and a more practical deference to nature than she did in Loudon's amorphous design for a house ". . . calculated for being decorated with ivy and creepers."[3] Between the two there lies a difference of outlook which has an important bearing on Regency design. Loudon and the root-workers tried to get back to nature by, as it were, digging themselves into the landscape. Repton and the horticulturalists tried to do the same by camping in it. Where Loudon was a troglodyte, Repton was a camper. One's house tended to be a glorified version of the cave, the other's an elaboration of the tent, and this sense of impermanence is a real factor in Regency architecture: more particularly in the case of the country house. John Plaw's design for a cottage, which he suggests could be built on wheels, so that it "might be moved at pleasure," shows that Regency architects even considered the mobile house as a practical possibility.

But it was the actual idea of the house as a tent which made such characteristic contributions to house design. Repton, when he reflects on the "modern improvement, borrowed from the French, of folding glass doors opening into the garden," decides that the resulting effect in the room "is like that of a tent, or marquee, and in summer, delightful":[4] and it was this same effect which was aimed at in the design of the verandahs, porches and balconies which accompanied the french window. Their characteristic "Chinese" covering is very much of a tent form interpreted in architectural materials. The connection can be clearly

<hr/>

[1] W. F. Pocock: *Architectural Designs for Rustic Cottages, Picturesque Dwellings, Villas etc.* (1807).
[2] J. B. Papworth: *Rural Residences* (1818).   [3] *Country Residences* (1806).
[4] *Fragments on the Theory and Practice of Landscape Gardening.*

seen in J. B. Papworth's design for an umbrella protection to a garden
seat (46), which is constructed of copper on an iron framing. It is
further emphasized by his inclusion of a design for a garden tent (47)
in the same book.

Tent-like decorations are a sufficiently familiar feature of Regency
architecture. Their use was, however, much more than an arbitrary one.
It represents a definite view of the house's connection with the garden.
This is shown, above all, in the design of the Brighton Pavilion, a
building which illustrates the final reconciliation of the Regency house
with its surroundings. It is from this point of view that the Pavilion is
such a representative building, and it is the one point of view from
which this much criticised design has been insufficiently considered.

Repton's part in it is well known, and how, in spite of the Regent's
assurance that he would have "every part" of Repton's design "carried
into immediate execution,"[1] the work was finally handed over to Nash.
But, although Repton learnt at such cost not to put his trust in princes,
much of the character of his design persists in Nash's building, while
Aiton's landscaping of the garden has probably worn better than Repton's
rather feeble formality would have done. The original idea was to make
an all-the-year-round garden, lavishly equipped with trellised walks,
aviaries and the other paraphernalia of the Regency garden. Among
them was an orangery (31, 32), whose windows and roof could be
removed and replaced by hanging drapery, so that the building could
be used as a garden "Chiosk" in the summer months. The idea is an
interesting one, as it suggests just that feeling for the building as a
tent-like structure which was to be developed by Nash in the design
of the Pavilion itself. The whole building could be imagined to be
supported by a series of posts: two great poles for the end pavilions,
from which the roof falls down as drapery might do; and a series of posts,
for the colonnades, with lace-like tracery hanging between them (45).
When he looked out of the ranges of french windows, the victim of
Prinny's overworked stoves had more reason than his own discomfort
for imagining that he was in a "marquee." He was, in an architectural
sense, actually in one. The mere fact that the chief patron of Regency
architecture should elect to house himself in a pavilion rather than in a
palace is a not unimportant commentary on this aspect of the Regency
house.

In following out the landscapists' arguments, and in adapting itself to
their gardens, the Regency house had in fact come very far from the
Palladian standards from which it had set out. The Pavilion is an extreme
case, as are the various efforts at Picturesque planning which have been
referred to. They represent the advance guard of an expeditionary
advance into the landscape whose main body had remained at the
Georgian base. But even the stragglers, most of them, derived some
advantage from the victories won by the vanguard; even laggards like
the "Improved" Littlebrain Castle generally acquired some new feature

---

[1] John Loudon: *Biographical Notice of the late Humphry Repton, Esq.*

in the form of a trellis, balcony or a french window. Considered in these terms the cult of the Picturesque garden was helping to make the country house of the Regency an infinitely more pleasant place to live

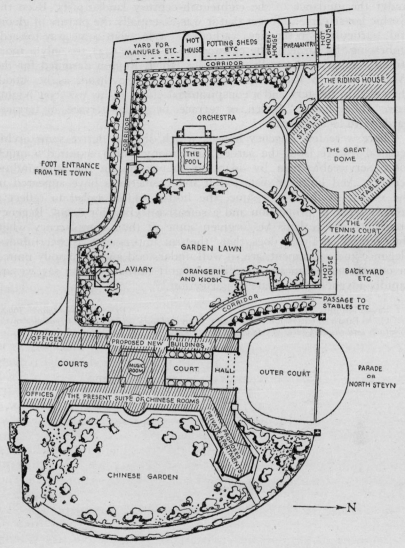

REPTON'S PROPOSED PLAN (1808)
FOR THE LAYOUT OF BRIGHTON PAVILION

in than its Georgian prototype had been. As Repton showed in his comparison between the "Ancient Cedar Parlour" (48) and the "Modern Living Room" (49), a good deal of restriction had gone out of the french window and a considerable amount of cheerfulness had come in by way of the conservatory. The balcony and verandah too gave on to a garden which was much nearer to the true sense of the "pleasure ground" than the "one dull, vapid, tranquil scene"[1] which had swallowed it up under the guidance of the eighteenth-century landscapists. Even the Gothic house came to forget that it was essentially the picture of gloom and, particularly in the airy "cathedral" style, went some way towards embracing the garden. The cloisters of Ashridge (44) are only a more stilted version of the trellised arcades which Repton designed for the White House in Richmond Park; and even Scythrop, as he stood, shrouded in mystery and a conspiratorial cloak, in his tower at Nightmare Abbey had a "garden, or terrace, or garden-terrace, or terrace-garden" to look out on.[2]

There were few Regency houses which did not derive some architectural feature from the garden, and many which acquired a much more serviceable plan by adapting themselves to the surrounding scenery. And however distorted it may sometimes have appeared in the mirror of the Picturesque, the house seldom failed to reflect a comely sense of proportion and a sensitive feeling for detail. Regency architects can perhaps be forgiven some of their complacency when they remark, as Busby does, that "the true impressions of cheerfulness, elegance and refinement, are so well understood and so happily united in our modern domestic dwellings, that I hesitate not to say we are rapidly advancing to a state of perfection."[3]

[1] Payne Knight: *The Landscape*.   [2] Peacock: *Nightmare Abbey.*
[3] C. A. Busby: *Designs for Villas and Country Houses (Adapted with economy to the Comforts and the Elegances of Modern Life)* (1808).

III

Taste and Technique

THE "Man of Taste" might well congratulate himself as he saw the Regency house beginning to take shape in conformity with his theories. For, quite apart from its aesthetic merits, it was, as a pleasant and workable "home," something far in advance of the standards set by its Georgian predecessor. For this achievement he may be allowed to take much of the credit. He should certainly not be allowed to take it all. Quite as much is due to the technician, whose conscientious study of materials and building technique contributed almost as much towards the Regency Style as did the theories of the "Man of Taste."

Regency architecture is, more than anything, the product of these, often conflicting, influences. In it theory had to be reconciled with practice, taste with technique. The tax on windows and the glimpse of a Picturesque prospect were considerations of almost equal weight in determining the form of the house. The repeal of the Laws of Apprenticeship had almost as far-reaching an effect on its decoration as Denon's travels in Egypt or Daniell's in India. Sometimes practical considerations even suggested the direction in which taste was to develop. An instance of this is the design of balconies in town houses. At one time a law forbidding their projection over the pavement threatened to eliminate balconies altogether in the town house. They were, however, generally permitted by local surveyors on condition that they were designed with a sufficient appearance of lightness, and this necessity became the mother of Regency architects' inventiveness in devising light decorative balcony forms.

There was one practical consideration above all which affected the trend of contemporary taste. It was one which was implicit in the early nineteenth-century background of England's rapid commercial expansion, and, as an influence on architectural appearances, it took the form of a changeover from craftsmanship to factory production. For industry was not only producing new building materials. It was also producing them in a new way, which, whether they liked it or not, architects had to take some account of. Architects whose traditions of practice had been built up on the limited range of materials available were now faced with the use of new materials, with no traditional precedent for applying them. For these were materials whose final appearance was no longer decided by the individual touch of a craftsman, but by the standardising stamp of the machine. How was this new factor of "massproduction" to be reconciled with the canons of contemporary "Taste"?

47

This was one of the most important of the questions which contemporary conditions forced the Regency architect to answer.

To the majority of them the reply seemed obvious enough. The machine was a heaven-sent answer to the demand for taste. It was not only sent so that they might have taste, but that they might have it more abundantly. By means of it, "works of the most refined and delicate character, which, executed in the usual expensive materials, could have exercised a refining influence over the minds of the few only, have been, and may be, so generally disseminated, as to enter into the household existence and daily associations of the larger portion of the educated community." Such at least was the opinion of the manufacturers of "Jackson's Papier Mâché Ornaments," whose pattern books show a typical use of machinery to imitate the craftsman's ornament. But more important even than the "general dissemination" of taste which these products made possible was their ability to do so cheaply. As Jackson's pattern book points out, they were ". . . ready for immediate application at a defined and economical cost, which the tedious process of designing and modelling prevents, as well as the great saving of time that results from employing those products that are ready, or that can be supplied at a speed equal to any requirement."

These were arguments which were particularly telling at a time when skilled labour was hard to come by owing to the increasing number of men employed on government work, such as barrack building, and when war conditions had sent the cost of building materials soaring. As a means of eliminating "the tedious process of designing and modelling" these materials were therefore welcomed, not only by speculative builders but by many of the most reputable architects of the Regency. Jackson's pattern book of 1849 mentions Nash, Smirke, Blore, Hardwicke, Barry, C. R. Cockerell and Benjamin Wyatt as clients; while an example quoted (and illustrated) with special satisfaction is Smirke's decoration of the "Egyptian Hall" in the Mansion House.

The success of the papier-mâché ornament is typical of the advance of "mass-production" at the expense of craftsmanship, an advance which is symbolised by the repeal of the "Laws of Apprenticeship" in 1813. The machine and its idiosyncracies could no longer be denied as a factor in architecture. Many of its effects were deplorable, but in some cases it was made to contribute handsomely to architectural design. The highly standardised types of balcony railing (59), which were distributed all over England and often abroad, represent, for example, a notable contribution made by "mass-production" to Regency architecture.

There is one particular accompaniment to this "mass-production" of building materials which had an important bearing on Regency design, and that is the immense development of communications at the time: the large-scale road-making which was fostered by Macadam's legislation and made effective by Telford's improved methods of construction, also the hectic cutting of canals to keep pace with the expansion of industry. These, in themselves, encouraged significant adventures in structural engineering. They also made possible a rapid and widespread distribution of materials, and with them, of ideas as to how they should be used. The new roads and canals brought to the remote countryside materials, such as cast-iron balconies from Bersham and stock bricks from London, which foreshadowed the end of local building traditions. They also brought sophisticated notions of the Picturesque and a townsman's version of rural architecture which sprinkled the countryside with villas and ornamental cottages.

With Regency architecture there starts the period of a rapid levelling of architectural ideas. In remote quarters "local traditions" may have held their own, but a great part of the countryside fell before the advance of artificial standards of taste. The loudest praise for the use of "local materials" did not come from the places in which such materials still fostered special building styles: it came from the city offices of architects intent on exploiting the countryside as a playground for the "Man of Taste." Symbolical of the levelling of ideas which followed improved communications is the indiscriminate use of stucco, a material which was first used to solve a special architectural problem. For stucco, as Repton relates in the *Theory and Practice of Landscape Gardening*, was essentially a product of the seaside town. As a protection against strong winds and salt sea air it was a material of special value. But, once successfully used in this way, it soon began to spread a standardising veneer over the architecture of town and countryside: and, as was so often the case in Regency architecture, the essentially practical idea which first suggested its use came to be of less account than its associations with "correct taste," and particularly its aptitude for Picturesque design. In this connection it is important to realise that, like Jackson's "papier mâché" and so many of the building materials of the period, stucco was a substitute material. Its chief recommendation was that it could be used to imitate stone. Busby made the suggestion in connection with his design for an entrance lodge that "the whole should be stuccoed in imitation of stone"[1] and this was the point of view from which most enthusiasts for the material came to consider it.

An appearance of "richness" was generally considered to be a necessary accompaniment to the Picturesque, and stone was thought to be the ideal material for producing such an effect. Brick was conveniently out of favour among Regency architects for its alleged poverty of appearance, but with a stucco coating "in imitation of stone," it easily acquired some measure of respectability. Atkinson for one decides that "in consequence of the numerous small parts in brick-work, and the regularity of the courses, I should never use it where stone can be had."[2] In this case, however, the substitute suggested is not stucco, but brick walls dashed with quick-lime and sharp sand, and "coloured so as to imitate stone."

[1] C. A. Busby: *Designs for Villas and Country Houses* (1808).
[2] *Cottage Architecture* (1805).

I

That stucco was a material with a quality of its own and one with particular pitfalls and possibilities inherent in its use seems to have struck architects less than its value as a short cut to Picturesque effect. But, although it does not seem to have been consciously aimed at, an individual quality does show through many of the stucco subterfuges of Regency architects. The effects they were after in stucco design can be seen particularly clearly in the case of the many fine buildings in Cheltenham, where there is a free use of both stucco and stone. Papworth's "Lansdowne Terrace" (52) represents the ideal of the elaborate stone "terrace," well provided as it is with the "richness," "elaboration" and "tints variously broken and blended" which accompanied Picturesque design. Other Cheltenham terraces have been faced with stucco as a measure of economy, and, although they have set out to look like stone buildings, they have acquired, willy-nilly, a certain individual quality from the material they use.

Living, as we are, at a time in which new materials and the type of design they suggest have been studied to such immediate architectural effect, we may feel inclined to regret that Regency architects did not inquire more deeply into the individual qualities of their materials. But, although it may not have been a conscious one, there does exist a recognisable relationship between the design of the Regency façade and the use of stucco as a facing for it. And this indebtedness of design to material is, to some extent, a reciprocal one. Stucco was welcomed because it provided a pliable and cheap medium in which to realise the intricacies of the Picturesque. At the same time it is quite possible that its use helped to suggest the actual "style" of façades. For smooth, unbroken surfaces, although they are responsible for many delightful effects in Regency buildings, are apt to encourage staining and general deterioration of the walls. Experience of this taught architects to reserve the use of such surfaces for brick buildings. Carried out in stucco, the flutings, string courses and imitation stone joints of the "Grecian" style, or the all-over elaboration of the Gothic, made for a more effective "weathering" of surfaces, and the increasing reverence for the "Styles" during the Regency period may have been in some measure due to this fact.

Whatever the reasons, and there are no doubt many others beside the ones already suggested, stucco established itself as the fashionable material of the day. It was the one to which the villa and the terrace house looked alike for their crockets and their capitals. As evidence of the social standing associated with it there are numerous cases in which one house in a brick-built terrace has had its front stuccoed as a means of asserting its superiority over its neighbours.

Besides stucco there were a host of substitutes for the vaunted "richness" of stone. One such material was the variety of "patent stone" manufactured by Messrs. Coade and Seeley. Even such a stickler for purity of architectural principles as Sir John Soane was not above making use of it, and "enriched" the façade of his house in Lincoln's Inn Fields with caryatids cast in Coade and Seeley's stone.

63 Greek Motifs in a Plaster Ceiling at Pitzhanger Manor, Ealing. *Sir John Soane*, *Architect*

64 A Door in No. 25 Mecklenburg Square, London. *Joseph Kay*, *Architect*

65 A Staircase in a London house, similar to Soane's elegant design (66) at Moggerhanger

67   Waterloo Bridge (1811–17). *John Rennie, Architect*
From a print by T. H. Shepherd

68   Telford's Essay in "Keeping in Keeping" at Conway

Artificial stone was in fact widely recognised as a substitute for an original which was often expensive and hard to come by. Dearn, when in doubt about the practicability of one of his designs in what he calls the "abbey or church Gothic style," suggests that it might be carried out in stone—"principally, though artificial stone may be substituted with good effect, for the decorative parts."[1] The chief argument for the use of artificial stone was of course the one which endeared so many of the new industrial products to Regency architects, namely that it provided a means of mass-producing those ornaments for which contemporary taste was expressing a mass demand. "It may be nearly all composed of artificial stone," writes Thompson of his design for an "Aquatic Temple," ". . . in which material it would not be expensive on account of the number of ornaments that might be cast from the same mould."[2]

But although such questionable motives were admittedly uppermost in the minds of many architects using substitute materials, a serious study of the appearance and weather-resisting properties of materials is in evidence in much Regency architecture, and considered in these terms, they had by no means a negligible effect on its appearance. Brick, although it continued to be widely used, was in some disfavour, not only as being an unsuitable medium in which to execute Picturesque intricacies, but for the more telling reason that bricks were heavily taxed. One effect of this was that builders tended to fall back on wood construction in many country districts. The area in Kent and Sussex, for example, which includes such villages as Sandhurst, Hawkhurst and Peasmarsh, provides a variety of interesting wood cottages dating from the late eighteenth century and the Regency period.

Tile hanging was another traditional building form on which architects fell back, and there is many a house and terrace with a sophisticated stucco front, for whose back and sides the more economical method of tile hanging has been adopted. The well-known plaque affixed to the cottages in Barker's Place at Stonehouse, shows that there were even attempts to improve on the natural virtues of slating and tiling as cheap weather-resisting materials. Inscribed with the date, 1806, it records how "Phillip's patent method of slating and tiling below is his Everlasting Coating or Patent Weather and Fireproof Composition."

Another characteristic material, used like stucco originally for protecting buildings on exposed sea fronts, is the glazed brick. The Royal Crescent at Brighton is an excellent example, in which glazed bricks remain bright and undamaged in a position in which ordinary bricks would have rapidly deteriorated.

To place their buildings on exposed sites was a deliberate move on the part of many Regency architects. And when they followed Repton's advice and built on high ground, when they joined in the fashionable rush to the seaside, or when they built a house in some Sublime but

[1] T. D. W. Dearn: *Designs for Lodges and Entrances to Parks, Paddocks and Pleasuregrounds, in the Gothic, Cottage and Fancy Styles* (1823). [2] *Retreats* (1825).

windswept situation, the qualities of their materials were put severely to the test. The same is true of the "terraces" of houses, which in all possible cases, made the most of sites which gave them command of a wide range of scenery. It was not only on the cliffs at Brighton that architects had to keep a watchful eye on the effectiveness of their facing materials. Similar conditions applied on the downs of Clifton, the cliffs of Dover, the summit of Richmond Hill and on the innumerable other elevated sites which were considered ripe for Regency development.

Thus, while the Picturesque was preventing the technique of the iron-workers from getting rusty, the Sublime was, equally effectively, keeping the joiners up to the mark. Even if it enjoyed such a situation as Mrs. Radcliffe herself would have found congenial, a speculative terrace was likely to have a somewhat impaired letting value if its windows failed to keep out the accompanying gale. Good joinery was, from this point of view, another outcome of the reaction of technique on contemporary taste. With it there came such features as the double window. For in many Regency buildings sash windows were combined with casements so as to provide an effective form of weather-proofing. In towns this method also served to exclude street noise.

The use of the double window was even carried sufficiently far for it to suggest an elementary idea of air-conditioning, as is shown by Atkinson's rather nebulous suggestion for a system of ventilating flues used in conjunction with double windows. "These tubes," he claims "would at all times convey the corrupted air from the apartments without exposing the inhabitants to currents of cold air, or causing a waste of fuel to restore the lost heat."[1]

The design of windows underwent considerable changes during the period and the single large openings, which architects used more and more in place of the series of regular rectangles, made a marked contribution to the Regency style, and a great deal of thought went into their design, not only in relation to the prospects they were intended to frame, but also as the means towards an improved lighting of interiors. James Malton, for example, concludes a series of "Designs for Villas," most of them in fancy Gothic styles, with a serious study of window placing and design. As a result of his inquiry he is, as he says " . . . fully satisfied that an apartment is made cheerful by a sufficiency of light flowing in from a centre."

Considerations of this sort were leading Regency architects away from the typical Georgian interior, lit by windows symmetrically placed about centre piers, and at the same time they suggested such treatments as the splaying of window jambs which, according to Malton, "in a thick wall especially, possesses somewhat the advantages of a bowed light, or what is called a bow window." The latter, of course, was considered a highly desirable form of window, not only for Picturesque reasons but because ". . . in consequence of the inclined

[1] *Cottage Architecture.*

lights, the sides of the room, perpendicular to the window, are better lit than they possibly can be through square openings in the wall."

But, as with so many features of Regency design, windows would never have acquired the characteristic forms they did had it not been for technical improvements in their material. In the case of glass the larger panes, which improved processes of glass-blowing made possible, upset the tradition of the multi-paned window whose design the late eighteenth century had brought to such perfection. Mrs. Gaskell, writing in 1863, records how the windows of a shop ". . . had long since been filled with panes of glass that at the present day would be accounted very small, but which seventy years ago were much admired for their size,"[1] and such an admiration for the new "capabilities" of glass was general among Regency architects. "By means of glass," says John Britton, "we repell the inclemency of the elements, may be said to render our walls transparent, and can enjoy the distant prospect from our firesides. By the aid of mirrors we multiply the costly embellishments that surround us, extend the apparent dimensions of our rooms, and create the most magical effects." "What," he asks, "would the possessor of the most splendid palace of antiquity say, could he witness this species of luxury, of which he had not even an idea?"[2]

His reference to mirrors touches on another important aspect of the use of glass, for they were often used for deliberate architectural effect in interiors. Malton, while eliminating the central pier between windows, finds himself wondering where to put the mirror which generally filled this position. His conclusion that it should be placed instead "over the chimney-piece" was the one generally subscribed to by Regency architects. The enormous mirror in the Brighton Pavilion, reflecting 13 feet by 8 feet of "costly embellishments," shows this idea attaining monumental proportions. Britton's corrolary, that mirrors "extend the apparent dimensions of our rooms," also had a wide appeal for architects bent on the pursuit of Sublimity. Repton used them to exaggerate the length of his trellised walks, and they form a definite architectural element in Soane's interiors. In the case of Pitzhanger Manor their "magical effects" were so convincing as to prove a menace to those unfamiliar with Picturesque ideas. As the result of mistaking a pair of enfiladed mirrors for a corridor, a visitor to the library injured himself so severely that some of them were subsequently removed.

With glass, as with most of the materials used during the Regency period, scientific considerations were thus weighed against aesthetic ones to produce characteristic effects. In doing so, architects showed that proper sense of values which gives such vitality to their style. They talked a great deal about art, but they also thought a great deal about science. Many a Regency aesthete on closer examination turns out to be a scientist in disguise.

Joseph Gwilt, when he was awarded the first premium for the design

[1] Elizabeth C. Gaskell: *Sylvia's Lovers.*
[2] John Britton: *The Unity of Architecture, Painting and Sculpture, etc.*

of a new London Bridge in 1823, did not win merely on the aesthetic merits of his design. He also won on the practical knowledge which had enabled him to write, twelve years earlier, a treatise *On the Equilibrium of Arches*. J. W. Hiort, as Clerk to the Board of Works, was, in practice, mainly concerned with such subjects as the decorations for Pitt's funeral and Nelson's, the celebrations for George IV's fiftieth birthday and for his coronation; but his knowledge of architecture went much deeper than its mere trappings. The construction of chimneys was his special subject. He published a treatise on their design, invented a patent brick for building flues, and formed a company, the "London, Surrey and Kent Safety Brick Company," to manufacture them. Similarly the architect William Atkinson was not only the pioneer of Gothic revivalism who built Abbotsford for Sir Walter Scott. He was also a competent chemist, geologist and botanist, and made a useful contribution to Regency building materials in the form of a stucco called, after its inventor, "Atkinson's Cement."

An infinite number of such examples could be quoted, but these few are sufficient to show that Regency architects were far from functioning, as it were, in an aesthetic void. The Picturesque and its appropriate expression in architecture was their ruling passion, but they did not give themselves up to it without making some acknowledgment to the scientific trend of the times. For many of them the products of industry had as much fascination as the products of nature, and considerations of "utility" applied equally to the heating of a house and to the planting of its garden.

Their enthusiasm for practical things is inclined to take the form of an emulation of the "gadget" and the "patent," but in many cases this scientific outlook contributed both to the workability and to the appearance of Regency buildings. It at least provided an architectural anchor at a time when aesthetic theories were drifting very wide of a practical mark; above all it produced a frame of mind in which technical improvements were welcomed by architects and serious efforts made to reconcile them with their notions of design. The welcome given to gas lighting generally and the examples, such as Brook's library in the Royal Institution, in which the gasoliers made a handsome contribution to the interior design, is in striking contrast to architect's initial failure, a century later, to treat electricity in the architectural way in which it should have been treated.

It was in the design of theatres that gas came to the fore as a practical method of lighting, its use spreading from the stage to the auditorium itself, and it is in the theatre interior that the technical side of Regency architecture is seen to particular advantage. In lecturing to his students, Soane did not mince words about Smirke's design of Covent Garden, but his contemporaries were prone to overlook deficiencies in its external appearance as they hurried inside to contemplate the "magnificent chandelier," which is described as "diffusing a soft and brilliant light around, without obtruding the view of a single spectator."

69 A typical Greek design by Robert Smirke: The College of Physicians, Trafalgar Square (1824-7)

70 University College, London (1827). *William Wilkins, Architect*

From Shepherd's "Metropolitan Improvements"

71 Chester Castle (1783–1830). A General View. *Thomas Harrison, Architect*

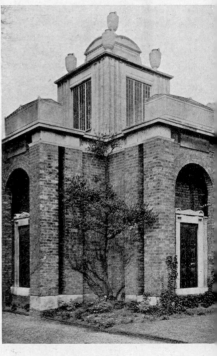

72 Chester Castle: an Interior

73 The Mausoleum, Dulwich Colleg
(1811–14: destroyed 1944)
Sir John Soane, Architect

REGENCY MONUMENTAL

And in the same theatre there was equal applause for the decoration of the auditorium and for its method of "forced ventilation" and heating by "Calorifere Fumivore Stoves."

It was in fact as great a recommendation for the architect that his decorations reflected all the attributes of the Picturesque as that the interior could be "either Cooled or Warmed, and the atmosphere of the different Parts of the House can be kept to one pleasant Temperature throughout the different seasons of the year."

The Regency's pioneer efforts in central heating are alone a monument to architects' ability to make capital of the new equipment with which industry was providing them. Soane, who considered the "due, and equably warming of rooms in cold climates" to be ". . . of great importance to the health and comfort of the inhabitants of every dwelling, from the Cottage of the Servant to the Palace of the Sovereign," pays tribute to the "labours and talents of Messrs. Boulton, Watt and others" under whose guidance ". . . Steam has been most usefully and successfully applied, not only in our Manufactories, but likewise for the warming of Apartments of different magnitudes."[1] The steam heating system which he installed in his own house was a practical gesture in favour of his verdict that "Perhaps for the Halls, Galleries, Corridors and such like parts of our Houses, no mode yet discovered has been more safe, economical, or better adapted for the purpose."

It was again in the theatre that significant efforts were made to tackle the problem of fire-resistance which, in turn, to some extent influenced the architect's choice of building materials. The epidemic of fires which swept the Regency theatres is commemorated in a piece of contemporary doggerel, describing how

> Base Bonaparte, filled with deadly ire,
> Sets one by one our playhouses on fire.[2]

Robert Smirke, as the architect appointed to rebuild Covent Garden Opera House, was, however, less inclined to place the blame for the fire which had destroyed it in 1808 on Bonapartist sabotage than on the inflammability of its material. He accordingly called in Sir Humphrey Davey to give his advice on fireproofing the new building, but the fact that Smirke's theatre itself eventually succumbed to a fire is not a convincing advertisement for Sir Humphrey's methods.

[1] Sir John Soane: *Lectures on Architecture.*

[2] Some years ago he pounced with deadly glee on
The Opera House, then burnt the Pantheon;
Nay, still unsated, in a coat of flames
Next at Millbank he crossed the River Thames,
Thy Hatch, O Halfpenny pass'd in a trice
Boiled some black pitch and burnt down Astley's twice;
Then buzzing on through ether, with a vile hum
Turn'd to the left hand fronting the Asylum,
And burnt the Royal Circus in a hurry—
'Twas called the Circus then, but now the "Surrey."
(Rejected Adresses, 1812).

Smirke, in common with many Regency architects, was probably inclined to put too great a faith in iron as a fireproofing material. Hartley's patent system of nailing iron plates to the structural carpentry of houses is typical of architects' misdirected energies in this direction. What, however, might be described as a pioneer of modern methods of fireproofing was the system evolved by Benjamin Wyatt and Colonel Congreve for Drury Lane Theatre (9). An elaborate "sprinkler" system covered the galleries while, in the decoration of the "Pit Ceiling," fireproofing was pressed into the service of taste in the form of a fitting described as an "Apollo's Head," which worked "upon the same principle of action as the fire-work, called the Catherine-wheel."[1]

From this, as from many other points of view, Wyatt's theatre is a landmark which stands out significantly from the common run of Regency designs. The published description alone is sufficient to show what a remarkable piece of architecture it was. It shows particularly the amount of practical thought which went into the planning of such buildings. Circulation and exits are carefully considered: a study of lines of vision suggests the horse-shoe formation of the auditorium which Wyatt claimed to be the first architect to adopt: acoustic diagrams (however suspect they may appear in the light of modern knowledge) are conscientiously worked out. The accompanying description of "the form or shape of the Theatre," as being derived from a study of "the primary objects of Distinct Sound and Vision" in itself shows a proper realisation that Picturesque ideas must be built up on a sound scientific basis if they were to acquire any real architectural merit.

Although architects subscribed willingly enough to romantic notions of "Style" they seldom lost their heads over them, and a large measure of their enthusiasm was still reserved for the more practical aspects of design. To adopt the "Style" of a previous age, in architecture, dress or even in thoughts or manners, was one thing. To consider dispassionately the products of their own day was quite another. To-day it is difficult to understand that these two outlooks could be considered anything but incompatible. But the Regency did not necessarily find them so. This helps to explain such paradoxes as that a man as far gone in romantic architecture as Sir Walter Scott could reserve his greatest enthusiasm for a subject so eminently lacking in its attributes as Telford's aqueduct at Pont-Cysylltau. It was, he decided, "the most impressive work of art he had ever seen."[2]

Thus, the men who expended so much effort in interpreting the Picturesque often gave the full measure of their approval to structures that were not Picturesque at all and to the many remarkable products of straightforward engineering design. The reconciliation of the romantic view of architecture with the strictly utilitarian one had an important part to play in Regency architecture. For, in so far as the two were reconciled, they defined the outline of an individual building style.

[1] Benjamin Wyatt: *Design of the Theatre Royal, Drury Lane* (1813).
[2] Letters to Southey.

Strictly speaking there is no Regency "Style." There was no universally accepted formula for design; there was scarcely even a general agreement as to what the architect's aims should be. There is, however, a tendency towards establishing an individual style which resulted from the balancing of these distinct points of view. To the left architects looked towards those utilitarian designs which applied new materials and forms of structure to such remarkable effect. To the right they looked towards the aesthetic tangle of Picturesque architecture. Most of them inclined to one side or the other. There were very few who realised that the way towards a Regency style lay straight ahead: that progress towards an appropriate formula of design was a matter of keeping in view the principles suggested by Picturesque theory while not losing sight of those forms which new materials and methods of structure were suggesting. The Picturesque could never be anything but a veneer. It needed a framework of sound structure to support it. Both in a figurative and in a concrete sense Regency design relied on a clear expression of structure.

At the time, structural materials were literally in the melting-pot; for, as iron became established as a reliable and economical form of structure, architects had to think seriously about the way in which they were going to use it. There were few architects of note who did not apply the material in some form to the construction of their buildings. Nash's grandiose façades and his palatial interiors were very much dependent on its use and his study of its properties was even sufficiently serious for it to lead him to take out a patent for a new type of iron bridge. Smirke's designs, particularly his large box-like interiors like the King's Library in the British Museum, owe much of their impressive effect to their iron structure. Sir John Soane was, as his "Academy Lectures" show, something of an enthusiast for its virtues, particularly as a fire-resisting material. "Is it not painful to observe," he says, "Walls of Thirty or even Forty Feet high, in some of the most populous situations, supported on the most paltry Timber mechanism, when they might be so easily charged on Iron Cradles with Iron Columns under them?"

There were even such parallels with the enthusiasm for new structural materials to-day as the houses, formed entirely of cast iron, which were advocated by John Wilkinson, the "Iron Madman." Wilkinson did in fact find his final home in an iron coffin which, during his lifetime, he was in the habit of showing to his guests as a form of after-dinner entertainment: to which Sublime spectacle the ladies among them would show a proper sensibility by fainting clean away.

But John Wilkinson was much more than an eccentric with a taste for the fashionable macabre. He was an engineer with a remarkably successful record in applying iron to shipbuilding and other forms of civil engineering, and it was the pioneer work of men of his profession which set the pace for the architect's use of the new material.

A consideration which helped considerably to familiarise them with

K

its use was that the present distinction between architecture and engineering was one which hardly existed during the Regency period. The men who designed the bridges, harbours, docks and canals in which iron was being so extensively and successfully used had not been trained to civil engineering as a profession. Even the existence of such a profession was as yet hardly realised. The greatest of the exponents of iron structure, Thomas Telford, was in fact an architect by inclination and a stoneman by profession. He was actually employed by Sir William Chambers on Somerset House, and Robert Adam helped him in his first steps towards an architectural career. The work of an engineer who, like Telford, professed to have "a tolerably general notion of architecture," could hardly fail to be appreciated by contemporary architects. When, in 1818, they saw him bridging the 1,700-feet span of the Menai Strait while, twenty years earlier, it had been considered something of an achievement to bridge even the smallest rivers satisfactorily, the time had clearly come for architects to take some account of the material in which it was done. Iron was found to be as effective in spanning large interiors as it was in spanning rivers, and its use for this purpose was carried very far by Regency architects. Good examples of this are the roofs of Foulston's public buildings at Plymouth[1] (81), while an interesting specialised type is the flat roof formed on an iron framework used by John Fowler for the Hungerford Market, and later in his own house.[2]

In adapting iron to their own uses architects not only had the technical experience of the engineers to go on. They also had the powerful aesthetic precedent which these men had created. It was one which was bent, above all, on using the materials to hand in the most expressive way, and its method was to go straight to the root of a problem without any preconceived idea of Picturesque effect. Yet in its results it often beat the "Man of Taste" at his own high-handed game. Such was the case with Rennie's breakwater at Plymouth, which he carried out in opposition to a scheme of Jeremy Bentham's for a series of banks connected by 140 wooden towers. Rennie's more straightforward expedient of dumping as much stone into the sea as was contained in the Great Pyramid makes his effort a more worthy claimant to Sublimity than anything achieved by the builders of Gothic towers.

But if the "architect-engineers," as they were appropriately called, were Sublime by nature, their picturesqueness was much more of an acquired quality. In many ways it is regrettable that they did acquire it at all. On the other hand this fashionable flavouring shows up their ideas more clearly as contributors to the Regency style. The very fact that the aesthetic element was recognised in engineering made some acknowledgment of the Picturesque inevitable. The architect-engineers were men who were anxious that their works should be acknowledged

---

[1] Drawings and descriptions of these roofs are given in Foulston's *Public Monuments in the West of England.*

[2] A description, showing the care with which he studied the question of insulation, is given in the *Transactions* of the R.I.B.A. for the year 1836.

74. St. Pancras Church (1819–22).
W. and H. W. Inwood, Architects

75. St. Matthew's, Brixton (1822–4).
Ascribed to C. F. Porden

76. St. Marylebone Parish Church (1813–17).
Thomas Hardwick, Architect

LONDON CHURCHES

77   Eastnor Castle, Herefordshire: A "Gothic" Design developed from a Classic Plan. *Robert Smirke, Architect*

78   Panshanger, Hertfordshire: a "Gothic" House with "Grecian" Interior. (*"Country Life" Photograph.*) *William Atkinson, Architect*

as works of art, and their study of aesthetic theories was supplemented by direct contacts with architects and "Men of Taste." Telford's friendship with Southey and his connection with Archibald Alison, the author of *The Principles of Taste*, the fact that he was a voracious reader and even an aspirant to poetic honours, all suggested some acknowledgment to the literary point of view in his work. Many of his designs show accordingly a grafting of "Style" on to their structure in the spirit common to many of the "architect-engineers." An enthusiasm for mediaeval detail which he had acquired in his early stonemason days in Edinburgh bore fruit in a promiscuous sprinkling of castellated pepperpots on many of his bridges, while the necessity for "keeping in keeping" with the Gothic castle provided an excuse for dressing up his suspension bridge at Conway (68) in a similar style. In the design for another suspension bridge, at Clifton, there was, however, less provocation for an elaborate Gothic design in which attention to the Picturesque has obliterated all trace of his fine engineering aesthetic.

By the true devotee of the Picturesque iron could not fail to be considered something of an intruder. Edmund Bartell's contemplation of his ideal rural scene is, for example, rudely disturbed by an iron gate, whose presence he finds "is every way offensive; even the sound of its falling to is shrill, harsh and dissonant and disturbs the tranquillity of the scene."[1] But the eye at least would be less offended if such iron structures were dressed up, as Telford sometimes dressed them, in the trappings of a recognisably Picturesque style. When they did so architects at least took some account of the nature of the material in deciding that the Gothic provided the most suitable form of embellishment. "Lightness" was generally recognised as a desirable quality in building, and lightness was the common attribute of iron as a material and the Gothic as a style. Thompson goes so far as to recommend a light iron bridge as being more Picturesque than a stone one in a scene which he describes. "In flat grounds," he says, "it requires some effort to prevent erections of this kind appearing cumbrous and intrusive. In this case iron is admirably adapted to lighten their character, and if the approaches are well planted out, they help to improve and diversify the scene."[2]

Similar arguments applied to the house itself, and it is common to find a free use of iron in those Gothic houses whose "tall aspiring forms" were, as has already been described, considered appropriate on such "flat grounds." Window tracery particularly was more easily, and to many Regency eyes, more appropriately, modelled in iron than carved in stone. Throughout Porden's remarkable essay in the "cathedral style" at Eaton Hall (86) the windows were made in cast iron, and many similar examples might be quoted. St. George's Church, Birmingham, shows that even a conscientious antiquarian like Rickman was not above using a modern material to reproduce historical detail.

For, besides its structural virtues, iron had all the advantages of the

---

[1] Edmund Bartell, jun.: *Hints for Picturesque Improvements* . . .   [2] *Retreats.*

substitute material. "The manufacture of iron," writes a great exponent
of its use, J. B. Papworth, "has been greatly benefited by improvements
in casting it, by which the embossed parts are relieved from the moulds
with so much purity, that little labour is afterwards required to complete
the richest ornamental work in this metal, which is therefore performed
at a small expense compared with the execution of such work a short
time since; and as iron itself is now at a very reduced price, it may be
expected that richly embossed works will come into frequent use,
particularly as this metal is now so generally substituted for several
other materials, that the century may not improperly be called another
"iron age." Papworth's prophecy, "that richly embossed works will
come into frequent use," was to come only too lamentably true, and
he himself was largely responsible for its doing so. For his own work
shows both aspects of the use of iron: in his decorative details there is a
lavish exploitation of the improved methods of casting, and, in his
factory designs, a straightforward structural use of it which shows a
proper appreciation of the "architect-engineer's" aesthetic.

IV

Towards a Regency Style

THE way in which the "architect-engineers" sought an appropriate Picturesque flavour for their iron designs in Gothic forms gives a clue to much of the feeling behind the Regency "Styles." It has an informative parallel in the adoption of Greek forms for their stone buildings. As was the case with iron, many of their most successful designs in stone make a straightforward use of the material, taking little account of questions of style. Sir Thomas Thrywitt's development of Dartmoor Prison and the neighbouring village of Princetown, with Daniel Alexander as his architect, is one such example. For Alexander, who was loudly praised for his original structure in Maidstone Gaol, is one of those border-line cases between architecture and engineering whose work shows how ideas were passing from one school of thought to the other. The appeal of his buildings is more easily appreciated by way of the knowledge that Alexander was an intimate friend of the sculptors Flaxman and Chantrey. Payne Knight's facetious suggestion that the "sculpturesque" might be opposed to the "Picturesque" as an aesthetic category was one that was actually being followed out by the architect-engineers. It might even be claimed that Alexander shows a better appreciation of the sculptural quality of stone than Flaxman or Chantrey do of clay or bronze.

That this view of architecture was also held in more academic circles is shown by Soane's explanation to his students that a building ". . . must form an entire whole from whatever point it is viewed, like a group of Sculpture, and not be like some of our Houses, where one front is decorated and the other quite plain, nor like some designs, one front being Gothic, another Chinese, Egyptian or even Grecian."[1] This "sculpturesque" quality gives the work of the "architect-engineers" a particular character, at least so far as their work in stone is concerned. Many of them, like Alexander, considered that such a quality provided sufficient justification for their work, but many more added superficial concessions to the Picturesque, and in these cases the use of the sturdy Greek Doric Order is the rule.

It is a paradox, typical of the conflicting sources from which the architect-engineers derived their knowledge, that it should be Rennie, the millwright, who brought this type of stone design to such perfection while Telford, the stonemason, became the *pontifex maximus* of iron design. A comparison between the early design for Kelso Bridge

[1] R. A. Lectures.

and his perfection of a similar design in Waterloo Bridge (67) is sufficient to show the way in which Rennie mastered his material.

But, quite apart from its Picturesque associations, there were many aims among Regency engineers which were satisfied by the adoption of Greek detail, and which were shared alike by architects emulating this engineering tradition. One is the pursuit of precision. It is seen alike in the almost inhuman accuracy of the jointing in Rennie's bridges, and in the hard, metallic detail of buildings such as University College (70). The way in which Wilkins used a metal finishing to round off the design of the dome shows clearly this affinity between the stone and metal design of the Regency. Another motive common to architects and engineers was the emphasis on structure, which was given such a subtle architectural expression in the work of Soane; a third was the fact that the Greek style represented a standard of design which was comfortable to fall back on at a time in which romantic ideas were wiping out many of the guiding lines which the architect had relied on following. Rennie, when he built the dorically-inclined Bell Rock lighthouse in almost exact conformity with the standard which Smeaton had established in the Eddystone, showed an appreciation of a standard which was a necessary element in the engineering aesthetic. When Nash had the columns for his Regent Street colonnade cast in iron, he acknowledged, from however commercial a motive, the existence of similar standards in architecture. The rule-of-thumb methods of Greek design represented the nearest approach to such standards existing in the realm of the Regency styles.

The engineer's emphasis is on one aspect of the Greek style: on its "sculpturesque" quality. The architect's emphasis is on another, or rather on the many considerations which are bound up with "Picturesque" design. Between the two points of view lies that of the architect making the most of both worlds, and whose buildings often represent an original contribution to the Regency style.

The distinction between architect and engineer is, as the very coining of the phrase "architect-engineer" suggests, an arbitrary one, and this helps to bridge the gulf between their respective outlooks. In some cases architects and engineers worked in collaboration. They did so in the case of the cast-iron Southwark Bridge, which was designed by an obscure member of the Wyatt family, John Wyatt, in collaboration with Rennie and Weston. In other instances architects and engineers seem to have competed on equal terms, as they did in the design of the new London Bridge which was awarded to Rennie on a margin of one vote over a design by the church architect and bridge-builder James Savage. Also many engineering works were rounded off by features designed by architects in the appropriate Greek idiom. Rennie's Ramsgate harbour was in this way completed by the addition of a clock house, an obelisk commemorating George IV's crossing to Hanover, and the "Jacobs Ladder" steps: all designed by the architect John Shaw.

Whether the designers of certain utilitarian buildings are more

79　A "Summer House in the Turkish Style"

From Lugar's "Architectural Sketches" (1815)

80　A View of Sezincote, Gloucestershire, from the Garden. *C. R. Cockerell, Architect*

THE ORIENTAL AESTHETIC

81   The Town Hall (1822), Column (1824) and "Egyptian" Library (c. 1824)

82   The Royal Hotel, St. Andrew's Chapel and Terrace, Devonport (1811–13).

Both from "Devonshire Illustrated" (1829)

FOULSTON'S PLYMOUTH

correctly referred to as architects or as engineers is, however, a relatively irrelevant question. What is important is that this engineering idiom does exist in Regency architecture and that it considerably helped the development of a Regency style. There are many architects whose work is obviously influenced by the "sculpturesque" design of the architect-engineers and by their use of structure to architectural effect. It is seen particularly clearly in the case of Thomas Harrison. Besides the work which he carried out for such a variety of patrons as Pope Clement XIV, Lord Elgin and the Emperor of Russia, Harrison designed a number of utilitarian buildings in the form of bridges and gaols, a lighthouse and a number of monumental features similar to John Shaw's at Ramsgate. But it is his group of civic buildings at Chester (71) which show particularly clearly what splendid results could be obtained when architects worked out their designs according to the precepts established by the engineers. Scrupulous structural honesty in the use of stone was one of their first principles and, in conformity with it, Harrison is supposed to have used nothing but jointed stonework in these buildings.

Architects seldom showed such care when taking the leaves they did out of the engineers' book, and from this point of view, Decimus Burton's Calverley Market at Tunbridge Wells makes an interesting comparison with the Chester Buildings. It has the same splendid sculpturesque quality, but its structure does not bear such careful examination; for several of the columns are of cast iron, and the architrave is a makeshift of brick and iron with a stucco facing. The same might be said of much of the Greek Revival work of the Regency. The pursuit of scholarship was scarcely compatible with the thoroughgoing honesty of the engineers, if only because the "correct" reproduction of a Greek building in its proper materials was hardly an economic proposition. This difficulty was brought home in the case of the "Million" churches, the majority of which were designed in some version of the Greek revival style.

When the grant of a million pounds was made by Parliament in 1818 for building new churches, Soane advised fixing a price of £30,000 for each building, but the Bill as it was finally framed defined two classes of building, for which sums of £20,000 and £10,000 were fixed respectively. The amounts were clearly not enough for architects emulating the "richness" of Greek design. As a result most of them had to stop short at a Picturesque façade, as Roper did in the case of St. Mark's, Kennington. Some, as C. F. Porden did at St. Matthew's, Brixton (75), managed to produce a fairly elaborate tower feature for the money, but the remainder of the church generally has to suffer in consequence. The fact that one of the few Regency Greek churches which bears more than a casual Picturesque glance, the Inwood's St. Pancras Church (74), cost over £70,000 to build, speaks for itself. The serious Greek revivalist seems to have considered that his style was above the subterfuge of stucco, and the result is seldom either Picturesque or inspiring architecturally.

Perhaps the best interpretations of the Greek style are to be found in the Scottish cities, where there was a tradition of building in hard stone. Elsewhere the best that can be said of the style was that it provided a safe standard for the design of civic buildings. The worst that can be said of it is that it tended to reduce architecture to a dead level in which Wilkins's design for Grange Park (112) would serve equally well for a Pall Mall club house. There was a good deal of talk about "propriety" in adapting the Greek style, but it referred more often to questions of scholarship than to the actual suitability of the Greek formula for any particular type of building. The Orders were given some consideration from the point of view of the ideas associated with them. Thompson, for example, holds the opinion that "where opulence exists independent of rank and title, the matronly Ionic may be considered as the most legitimate style for a family residence":[1] but in general architects failed to discover in Greek architecture the Picturesque subtleties which they pursued with such zeal in the rival styles. Gandy was even reduced to the expedient of drawing Soane's new buildings in ruins to bring out the full flavour of their picturesqueness.

The "Society of Dilettanti," with its "Ionian Mission" of 1811, was unfortunately something of a wet blanket to the Greek revival of the Regency, which suffered from its dictatorship just as the Gothic was later to suffer at the hands of the Camden Society. There seems to be an almost mathematical ratio between architects' familiarity with Greek buildings at first hand and the dullness of their own designs. Sir Robert Smirke, braving with his brother Edward the terrors of Turkish banditry, as they measured up temples "with a Janissary, armed with a loaded musket on each side to protect them,"[2] represents the highwater mark of Regency enthusiasm in this direction. In his own designs Smirke also represents the muddiest shallows of the Greek revival style. At the other end of the scale, Sir John Soane's failure to get nearer to the fountain head of Greek architecture than the temples of Sicily seems to bear some relation to his lively and imaginative handling of Greek forms.

The Greek revival of the Regency is well on the way to the antiquarian dead-end of the Victorians. The Gothic, on the other hand, was still the happy hunting-ground of the emotionally inclined. The antiquarians were nevertheless creeping in. John Britton, probing further into the "Beauties of England and Wales," was publishing the results of his researches as the "Architectural" and the "Cathedral Antiquities of Great Britain." A refugee from republican France, A. C. Pugin, was producing his careful drawings of Gothic furniture and architecture and Carter was circulating Gothic scholarship in the lending libraries to the tune of his two hundred and twelve letters to the *Gentleman's Magazine*. Architects like Kendall, Cottingham, Blore and Rickman were also producing their respective versions of the "principles"

---

[1] Thompson: *Retreats*.
[2] Edward Smirke: at Meeting of the R.I.B.A. June 17, 1867.

83   The Gallery

84   The Music Room

Both from "The Royal Pavilion at Brighton," by John Nash (1824)

CHINOISERIE IN THE BRIGHTON PAVILION

85   A View from Ackermann's *Repository* . . . (1823)

86   The Drawing Room.   *From "View of Eaton Hall," by J. C. Buckler* (1826).
William Porden, Architect

A HOUSE IN "CATHEDRAL GOTHIC" WITH WINDOWS IN CAST IRON:
EATON HALL, CHESHIRE

which had animated Gothic architects: in spite of which, correctness of scholarship is hardly the strong point of Regency Gothic design. Parts of buildings were often taken as patterns; the vault of King's College Chapel was a favourite, and was used, for example, by Archibald Elliot in St. Paul's Episcopalian Chapel at Edinburgh, but even in the case of copies of this sort, the "correctness" of the completed building was not given very serious consideration. Thomas Plowman found nothing incongruous in reproducing Magdalen College tower to a scale two-thirds smaller than the original in the design of Church Hill Church near Chipping Norton.

Architecture depends as much on the demands of clients as on the inclinations of architects, and during the Regency period there was not the antiquarian clientele for Gothic design which the Society of Dilettanti had fostered in the case of the Greek style. Its beautifully lithographed plates were calculated to give subscribers to *The Unedited Antiquities of Attica* very definite ideas on the subject of correct Greek design. The subscriber to the lending library was likely to derive a somewhat vaguer notion of Gothic detail from such novels as *Saint Bartolph's Priory*, on which ". . . no longer frowned the nodding capital of a once Saxon battlement deeply overhanging the little painted embrasures of the stained casements."[1] How a casement could have embrasures, why capitals should be decorating a battlement, and just how appropriate these features were in a Saxon building: such questions remained largely irrelevant beside the emotional effect conveyed.

In conformity with this literary view of architecture, the amateur Gothic antiquarian was becoming a power in the land. At Gwyrch Castle, Hesketh was building himself a house according to his own idea of Edward I's castles, and Beckford was trying to stimulate Wyatt into some activity over his galleries for mediaeval specimens. But such a parallel with the collections of the Greek Dilettanti by no means implied equal scholarship in the design of the gallery itself. For, when it came to the design of the house, Wyatt was free to pick and choose among the Gothic "Styles" as he thought fit. The important question was the Sublimity of the finished product, its astonishing effects of height and the length of vistas through rooms; also the Picturesque associations suggested by its details.

The same holds true of the majority of Gothic houses. It was an attitude which was supported by there being, apart from the castle, no recognised precedent for the design of a Gothic house. The mock castle was all very well for clients who wished to have their zest for "antiquity" coloured by melancholy reflections; but not every admirer of the Gothic style was a Mr. Glowry, and architects themselves only considered the "castellated" style to be Picturesque in certain situations. Hence the variations, such as the "House Gothic," the "Cathedral Gothic" and the "Florid Gothic," in which the adaptation of church architecture to existing domestic standards could not fail to produce somewhat

[1] T. Horsley Curties: *Saint Bartolph's Priory* (1806).

L

"original" results. Loudon in his *Country Residences* describes no less than six of these Gothic "Styles": *Saxon Gothic* (Norman), *Irregular or Mixed Gothic, the Cathedral Style, the Quadrangular Style and the Turret Style.* The titles themselves suggest that it was less the pursuit

A STATUE GALLERY

From Thomas Hope's *Household Furniture and Interior Decoration* (1807).

of historical accuracy than of emotional associations which influenced the architect in his choice of a suitable style.

It was its theatrical effect as a "property" in the Picturesque scene which was the chief recommendation for the Gothic house, and architects often acknowledged this, as Atkinson did at Panshanger (78), by combining a Gothic exterior with an interior modelled on the more convenient lines of the "Grecian" style. Payne Knight set the seal of "true taste" on this procedure by adopting it in the design of his own house; on the success of which "experiment" he considered that he had every reason ". . . to congratulate himself . . . he, having at once, the advantage of a Picturesque object, and of an elegant and convenient dwelling." As a further point in favour of the composite house he quotes its being ". . . capable of receiving alterations and additions in almost any direction, without any injury to its genuine and original character."[1]

On this question of correct conformity with historical precedent, the Arbiters of Taste allowed architects considerable latitude. Payne Knight as a leading light in the "Society of Dilettanti" professed a proper appreciation of scholarship in Greek detail. At the same time he considers the style to be well suited to combine with others in the cause of Picturesque effect. For these measures he finds, as might be expected, ". . . such authorities as the great landscape painters." In fact he goes so far as to state that "The best style of architecture for irregular and Picturesque houses, which can now be adopted, is that mixed style, which characterises the buildings of Claude and the Poussins: for as it is taken from models, which were built piece-meal, during many successive ages; and by several different nations, it is distinguished by no particular manner of execution, or class of ornaments; but admits of all promiscuously, from a plain wall or buttress, of the roughest masonry, to the most highly wrought Corinthian capital: and, in a style professedly miscellaneous, such contrasts may be employed to heighten the relish of beauty, without disturbing the enjoyment of it by any appearance of deceit or imposture."[2] It is a fundamental point in Regency design that it is a style "professedly miscellaneous." The wildest eclecticism was justified in the cause of the Picturesque and there remained little but "Taste" to restrain the consequent "licentious deviations of whim and caprice" which Payne Knight admits that he encouraged by his suggestions for an eclectic style. Payne Knight can refer his readers to the landscape painters as authorities ". . . the study of whose works may at once enrich and restrain invention," but for the heretic architects, who would not accept the dogma of picture-painting in architecture, there was no such authority to fall back on.

This need for an authority to guide their eclectic tastes was largely responsible for that study of the "principles" animating historical styles which, more than anything, holds Regency architecture together. Most styles were welcome as contributors to the Picturesque ideal, but they only acquired real architectural respectability if the "principles" behind them fell in with Regency motives. This emergence of the cult of "utility" in a new guise is recognisable in many romantic designs. Thus Robinson, in designing a series of village buildings in conformity with Price's ideas on the Picturesque, takes pains to find a practical justification for his use of the Swiss style for the "Market House and Shambles." The argument is that "The Swiss character is well adapted for a structure of this description, as the overhanging roofs afford considerable protection to the Stalls in bad weather."[3] Similarly Robert Lugar who

[1] Payne Knight: *Analytical Enquiry.* [2] Ibid.
[3] P. F. Robinson: *Village Architecture.*

"for the sake of variety" includes in his *Architectural Sketches for Cottages, etc.* two designs "In the Egyptian or Turkish Taste," finds a slender justification for adapting the latter to the design of a "prospect tower" (79). This "minarett," he contends, "if built in an appropriate situation, would prove an excellent landmark."

It might be pointed out as being one of the reasons for the eclipse of the Chinese taste at a time when it might have been expected to blaze in unprecedented glory that Regency architects never discovered any clear principles governing its design. To the eighteenth century the Chinese style had spelt fantasy and an outlet from the rigidity of Palladian rule. It was its chief recommendation that no principles of design were involved. In Regency architecture, the positions occupied by reason and romanticism were reversed. The fantasy which had lurked in the eighteenth-century background became the order of the day, with "principles" providing a necessary check on the consequent vagaries of taste. There was enough of fantasy in Regency architecture already, without the negation of principle implied in the Chinese taste. Hence even a patron who derived his taste so much from the eighteenth-century tradition as the Prince Regent did, needed some stimulant for adopting the Chinese style. Had it not been for the present of some pieces of Chinese wallpaper, he might never have decided to round off the Pavilion with Chinese decoration and furnishing (83, 84).

With travellers and archæologists following in the wake of imperialism, an assortment of far-flung styles was being brought home as potential contributors to an eclectic Picturesque style. Among the most notable of these were the Indian and the Egyptian styles. Denon, and the archæologists who followed Napoleon on his Egyptian campaign had introduced the style to the French Empire, and by way of the normal aesthetic channels it had spread to England. Thomas Hope, who had studied Egyptian architecture at first hand, set the seal of Dilettanti approval on the style when he domesticated it in the design of some of his "Household Furniture." Added to which recommendation, authors as widely read as Beckford and painters as popular as John Martin found the style to be one of unexceptionable Sublimity. Nevertheless few halls of Eblis and few exteriors in the form of Martin's Egyptian fantasies materialised in Regency architecture. The versatile Robinson adapted the style for the famous Egyptian Hall in Piccadilly, where Edward Bullock made capital of the Regency's interest in nature's whimsies by exhibiting the original Siamese Twins. Foulston, who, like Robinson, prided himself on his ability to express the Picturesque in terms of any given style, built an Egyptian public library at Plymouth (81), which was accompanied by a Greek town hall and an Indian chapel. But, apart from a few such examples, the Egyptian style seldom got beyond the cabinet maker, the interior decorator or the architect advertising his versatility in pattern-book projects. The failure of architects to produce any definite "principles" governing its forms was against a wider adaptation of the style. Elmes, for example, cautions

87 A "Small Villa in the Gothic Style"

88 A "Swiss Cottage designed as an entrance to a Park"

From "Domestic Architecture" (1833)

ROMANTIC DESIGNS BY FRANCIS GOODWIN

89, 90 Blaise Hamlet, Gloucestershire: a Group of nine *Cottages Ornées* (1809)
From contemporary prints
RUSTIC DESIGNS BY JOHN NASH

his readers that ". . . Although the lively Frenchman Sonnui says, that before it 'the so much boasted fabrics of Greece and Rome must come and bow down'; yet, when it is calmly investigated and brought to the test of judgment, it will not bear a momentary comparison with either, for chasteness, real beauty or true sublimity."[1] Some architects were more outspoken and Busby goes so far as to say that "of all the vanities which a sickly fashion has produced, the Egyptian style in modern architecture is the most absurd."[2]

AN EGYPTIAN ROOM
From Thomas Hope's *Household Furniture and Interior Decoration* (1807).

The Indian style, however, which had nothing more than the wistful thinking of retired civil servants and Daniell's plates to recommend it, had an influential analyst of its "principles" in the person of Humphry Repton. Repton's explanation of the derivation of Hindu forms from corbelling in rock was calculated to appeal not only to the cave-man in the Regency "Man of Taste." It even convinced the Prince Regent himself who, after he had seen the results of Cockerell's and Repton's concerted efforts to interpret the style at Sezincote (80), ordered Repton to prepare a scheme for indianising the Brighton Pavilion forthwith, with what disappointing results to the analyst of its "principles" is sufficiently well known.

Daniell's prints had many admirers among Regency architects, among them Robert Lugar, who acknowledges them as the source of his design

[1] James Elmes: *Lectures on Architecture* (1823).
[2] C. A. Busby: *Designs for Villas and Country Houses* (1808).

M

for a villa "In the Eastern Style." "It is but justice," he says, "to
acknowledge I have taken the idea of this design from one of Mr.
Daniell's views of India."[1] It would be more just still to say that Lugar
had merely pillaged some features of doubtful Picturesque value from
Daniell's books: in face of which Repton's attempts to determine the
"principles" underlying the style show up to advantage in the design
of Sezincote.

Repton's Indian "principles" are most in evidence in the garden
features, but in the design of the house as well he appears to have
made some suggestions as to how Hyder Ali Khan's Mausoleum at
Laulbaug should be adapted to the Cotswold scene. But although, as
he says, he gave his opinion "concerning the adoption of this new style,
and even assisted in the selecting of some of the forms from Mr. T.
Daniell's collection, yet the architectural department at Sezincote, of
course, devolved to the brother of the Proprietor." In a final compromise
with "convenience" Cockerell made use of the principles which Payne
Knight considered to be perfectly *en règle* in the case of the Gothic
style, and carried out the interiors in his normal classic manner. The
final effect, as recorded in the series of engravings by the Sublime
John Martin, is something of a vindication of the Regency's attention to
"principles" in adapting the planning of the house to the garden layout.
It also justifies the pursuit of "originality" as being a means of keeping
the veneer of style apart from the solid core of architectural design.

For Lugar was perfectly sincere when he considered that his design for
a Hindu house was "by no means unsuitable to an English Villa."
Architects had a sound idea of how a convenient house should be
planned, so far as questions of prospect and aspect and of the arrangement of interiors were concerned; and, when they chose to dress up
these essentials in the manner of mediaeval England or seventeenth-
century India, they were confident of their ability to give the style a twist
which made it "appropriate" to their own time.

Payne Knight, as a leading light in the Society of Dilettanti, was
among those who speeded Gandy, Gell and Bedford on their "Second
Ionian Mission" with the reminder to "exercise the utmost accuracy
and detail in your architectural measurements; recollecting always that
it is the chief object of the Society to promote the progress of architecture by affording practical assistance to the architects of this country,
as well as to gratify a general curiosity affecting the interesting monuments of antiquity still remaining in those parts."[2] The idea that
architects should abjectly copy the results of such Dilettanti labours
was nevertheless far from being his intention. Copyism was advancing
apace, and the publications of the Society of Dilettanti were one of the
chief causes of the Greeks being the first of the stylists to fall into the
antiquarian trap. Nevertheless the "Finger of Taste" was not inten-

---

[1] *Architectural Sketches for Cottages, Rural Dwellings and Villas, in the Grecian,
Gothic and Fancy Style* (1805).
[2] "Instructions to Mr. Gell and Mr. Bedford" (1811).

tionally pointing in this direction. Its arbiters ruled quite to the contrary: in fact that the "fundamental error of imitators in all the arts is, that they servilely copy the effects, which they see produced, instead of studying the principles, which guided the original artists in producing them; wherefore they disregard all those local, temporary or accidental circumstances, upon which their propriety or impropriety—their congruity or incongruity, wholly depend. . . ."[1]

That a house could, as Payne Knight recommends, "be adorned with towers and battlements and . . . still maintain the characters of a house of the age and country in which it is erected; and not pretend to be a fortress or monastery of a remote period or distant country"—this was a possibility which only an age over-confident of its taste could have envisaged. The attempts to live up to such a hopeless ideal do nevertheless give an air of individuality to the Regency styles which is lacking in the scholarly counterparts of the Victorians.

By way of such dicta the Arbiters of Taste were doing their best to put the styles in some perspective, to point out the virtues of the Greek and to suggest effective ways of applying the Gothic. The study of "principles" was considered to be a necessary means to this end. Unfortunately, architects seem to have been rather vague as to what sort of principles they were trying to establish. Had they been content to analyse the structural principles behind the historical styles their conclusions might have been of considerably more value. As it was, they were inclined to credit architects of classic Greece or Mediaeval England with a "Taste" as artificially cultivated as their own, and to analyse their architecture in corresponding terms.

Thus Blore goes to considerable lengths to show Gothic architecture as a sort of petrified version of the plant and tree forms which provided a subconscious standard for so much Regency design. It can, however, be said that the reading of such principles into the styles they copied helped Regency architects to capture the "originality" which they were so diligently pursuing. The leaven of Blore's Gothic "principles" is for example still working in the chapel he built as late as 1854 at Marlborough College. Here a highly individual version of Gothic form results from carrying out a vaulted roof in the only material which the slender buttresses are capable of supporting, namely wood boarding, on which the ribs are painted in perspective.

And, by way of considering the styles in terms of natural principles rather than structural ones, architects made some notable contributions to that pet Picturesque style of the Regency, the "Rustic" style. Repton, while he was on the subject of the "principles" governing Indian architecture, had also pointed out the origin of Greek structure in wooden posts and beams, and the associations which this idea suggested were made capital of by architects bent on evolving a "natural" style. Papworth, for one, records with approval how "The architects of the present day, attempting to combine fitness and beauty in rural buildings,

[1] Payne Knight: *Analytical Enquiry.*

revert to the above practices in the infancy of art, and, forming their
designs upon these simple models, gain some advantage by the association of ideas provided in the mind of the spectator, by its legitimate,
though distant affinity with the ultimate perfection of Grecian
architecture."[1]

Such cross-references to the inspiration which Gothic architects
were supposed to have derived from sylvan glades or to the "ultimate
perfection" of a Greek temple gave the final cachet which admitted
the Rustic style to the realms of Correct Taste. They gave an architectural validity to the rulings of such critics of the rural scene as
Edmund Bartell, that, for example, "trees of a proper size, in their
rough state, having only the bark taken off, are the most proper supports
for the cottage porch around which the ivy or the woodbine may be
trained, sometimes wholly, sometimes partially hiding these natural
columns, adorned by the varnished leaves of the one, or the gay and
luxuriant festoons of the other."[2] What materials should be appropriately used in these Rustic buildings and what principles should be
followed in designing them were questions on which Regency architects
expressed various and conflicting opinions. While True Taste, in the
person of Payne Knight, was inclined to frown on the style as being an
"affected" one, those architects who favoured it were indefatigable in
defining the exact "associations" appropriate to the style. Edmund
Bartell does not consider the subject of cottage design to be properly
covered until he has settled such details as that shutters are out of
character in a cottage because such a building is unlikely to attract the
burglar's attentions, or that fences composed of rakes and scythes
combined perhaps with "the irregular forms of the harrow, the hurdle
or the lift" would form an appropriate boundary for it.

Papworth, who, on Sir William Chambers's recommendation, had
been articled to that pioneer of the style, John Plaw, went further than
most architects in formulating treatments for Rustic buildings. Where
Bartell had been content to enumerate various local materials, including
the "indispensable" thatch, as being the proper ones for such buildings,
Papworth goes so far as to add the forms of the grotto-makers to the
"novel and fanciful effects" which the style is capable of producing.
Among them is included a recipe for a "stalactite wall" in which "coarse
sand and small pebbles of various sizes . . ." are "mixed up with Roman
cement diluted to the consistency of common rough-cast, and thrown
upon the walls in larger quantities than is usual: this is suffered to take
the irregular and projecting forms of stalactitae, those concoctions
resembling icicles that are frequently found in natural grottos."[3] So
much of "novelty" might seem to be enough, but the result is not
considered complete without the "fanciful effect" obtained by colouring
the stalactites "by tints representing them or by others that seem to

---

[1] J. B. Papworth: *Rural Residences* (1818).
[2] Edmund Bartel, jun.: *Hints for Picturesque Improvements* . . .
[3] *Rural Residences* (1818).

For such sticklers for the symmetrical as Busby the romantic styles had little appeal. The "principles" they followed were the strictly architectural ones which were implied in the classic tradition. Some concession might be made to the Picturesque in the detailing of the balconies and similar features which the Regency was making particularly its own. The basis of their style remained nevertheless the precept of Greece and Rome, and their individual designs were often close to the eighteenth-century tradition.

During the Regency, architects who followed the Roman precept were, however, relegated to the background. Sir William Chambers, for one, had seriously blotted the Palladian copybook when he gave what Payne Knight ironically describes as "equal proofs of the purity of his taste when he censured the temples of Athens and designed those of Kew."[1] A new "Italian" style was to appear towards the end of the period when G. L. Taylor applied the results of his studies of Italian architecture to the design of the south side of Gloucester Terrace, and even Soane finally adopted the style for his State Paper Office in Whitehall; but against the purity of Greek principles, the second-hand application of them in Roman architecture put the style at an obvious disadvantage.

Thanks partly to Soane, certain architects came to look on the reformed Palladianism of the Adam brothers as a possible contributor to a Regency style. The influence of their "principles" is seen in the work of James Wyatt, Holland and many lesser architects who gave their style an individual Regency twist. Architects in general seem, however, to have found their decorative detail to be in rather questionable taste.

The extent to which a study of "principles" in a Picturesque light was working for the eclipse of Roman architecture and the emulation of Greek and Gothic is shown by John Britton's reflections on the design of chimneys: ". . . the ancients," he argues "have left us no prototype for this indispensable part of a modern edifice; we may, however, rest assured that had they known the use of chimneys, they would have devised some means of rendering them not only pleasing but beautiful objects; for the pervading principle of their architecture—its first fundamental rule—was to render each part and feature subservient to decoration; even the very tiling of their roofs assumed Picturesque forms, and contributed to embellishment. The Italian school has proceeded on principles entirely the reverse, for it has carried mere originality to a disgusting excess, cutting up façades into 'bits of littleness' and gee-gaw trumpery so as utterly to destroy character, grandeur, proportion and simplicity. In this respect the architects of the style popularly designated Gothic, showed a far better taste: their doors and chimneys, in short, every feature, accorded with and formed a component part of the general design, but they were not copyists."[2]

[1] Payne Knight: *Analytical Enquiry.*
[2] John Britton: *The Unity of Architecture, Painting and Sculpture, etc.*

mark a lapse of time." Papworth is only able to record two instances in which his recipe has been used, but the less pretentious forms of "common rough-cast" seem to have been widely applied in Rustic buildings. So much consolation and much more, in the form of materials "left," according to Edmund Bartell, "from the hands of the carpenter," can the modern jerry-builder derive from Regency methods.

Its very closeness to nature, and hence to the heart of Regency taste, precluded any definite rulings as to what was the correct approach to the Rustic style. Such questions as whether it should be considered to be too unsophisticated for the "gentleman's Cot" and should be confined to cottages of a humbler order, split the ranks of architects designing in the style from top to bottom. The former was perhaps the more widely accepted ruling. On the other hand Nash's design for the Royal Lodge at Windsor shows that at least one architect of unexceptionable taste could bear even the sight of royalty relaxing under the thatched roof of a *Cottage Ornée*. The finer points of such arguments can be studied in the lively skirmishes which developed on the flanks of the "paper battle": for example in Richard Elsam's *Essay on Rural Architecture*, published in 1803, which the author describes as "being an attempt to refute, by analogy, the principles of Mr. James Malton's *Essay on British Cottage Architecture* (1789)."

The viewing of rural architecture in a romantic, picturesque light is characteristic of the Regency period; sufficiently so, at any rate, for it to have inspired a "studied crookedness" in all of Mrs. Rafferty's buildings and to have led her to observe that "uniformity and conformity, had their day; but now, thank the stars of the present day, irregularity and deformity bear the bell, and have the majority."[1] All the same, the advance even of Picturesque planning was being resisted at several points. Busby's remarks on the subject, for one, are worth quoting, as they suggest the fundamental differences of opinion which prevented the Regency from establishing any coherent style. "Some modern artists," he says, "have advanced as a maxim that the appearance of regularity in *rural* buildings should be studiously avoided; and they have endeavoured to draw a parallel between the productions of nature and the works of art. They say that the most beautiful aspects of nature are composed of irregular masses, and assemblage of light and shade; and that a similar and corresponding character should be given to everything which forms a part of the scene. This argument may at first appear plausible, but will not hold if we reflect, that in all landscapes where the building does not form a principal, the artists ought to consider that it forms only a *component* part of the scenery; and that all the beautiful effects of light and shade, of colour and outline, are produced by the contrast of the regularity of the building with the picturesque variety of nature; and it will be found that in such situations the most simple building will be the most pleasing."[2]

[1] Maria Edgeworth: *The Absentee.*
[2] C. A. Busby: *Designs for Villas and Country Houses* (1808).

95 Tyringham before the Alterations: an early house by Soane (1793–6)

96 Princes Street, Lothbury: a street façade designed by Soane (1808)

97 Interior of the Bank of England. The Entrance Vestibule from Princes
Street. *Sir John Soane, Architect.*

Reasoning of this sort contributed a good deal towards the elimination of undesirable styles at a time when architects were prone to embrace them all promiscuously. It is an essential part of that process of interpreting the "meaning" of architectural forms, which was the function of the Arbiter of Taste.

To the carefully cultivated palates of Regency architects Greek and Gothic meant a good deal: so, in some cases, did the Hindu, the Swiss, the Moorish and the Egyptian. The Roman, on the other hand, meant precious little until, in a ruined state, it acquired something of Sublimity and perhaps some vague associations with the Picturesque. If architects decided, like Busby, that it was "contrast" with the Picturesque scene that they wanted in a country building, or if they were confronted with a site which demanded a design on classical lines, it was, therefore, to the Greeks that they were likely to turn for inspiration. By many, in fact, the term "Grecian" was taken to be synonymous with classic design. In civic buildings, where considerations of this sort generally applied, the position of Greek architecture was almost unassailable, and there is hardly a town in England which did not acquire some civic building in the Greek style during the Regency period.

According to the "meaning" they wished to convey, architects drew on the repertory of the approved styles. Every architect was expected to be able to turn his hand at least to Greek and Gothic with equal facility, and it is a proof of the public's expectations of them in this direction that the most successful ones, such as Nash, Smirke and Wyatt, made almost equal quantities of designs in both styles. Soane is an exception, but Soane stands alone, both as an architect who achieved recognition in spite of almost constant public disapproval of his buildings, and as a man who saw that eclecticism should be less a matter of ability to command a variety of "Styles," than of uniting the "principles" behind them to form a contemporary method of design.

When it came to handing out the rival styles to order, Soane proved himself to be as ambidextrous an architect as any. He did so in the case of the Westminster Law Courts for which, by order of a Select Committee of the House of Commons, he produced a Gothic substitute for what had originally been a classic façade. But such a perfunctory response to the Picturesque runs counter to the spirit of Soane's "principles." He admired, and was not above making essays in, the Gothic style. His professed aim was nevertheless to adapt those of its "principles" which fitted in with his catholic view of architecture. The pendentive ceiling in his house in Lincoln's Inn Fields is more characteristic of his approach to the style than the elaborate tracery of the Stowe library. And he took the same view of many of the other architectural foibles of his contemporaries. His acknowledgement to the Sublime in incorporating the "Monks Parlour" in his London house and to the Picturesque in embracing some problematical ruins in the layout of

his country house at Ealing, both show that he took some account of
the literary views held at the time. His main intention was rather to
build his designs on the skeleton of such ideas: on the forms of structure
and planning they suggested. More clearly even than Payne Knight he
states his view of the function of the styles as being one of suggesting
"principles" of design rather than of providing subjects to copy. "We
must be intimately acquainted," he tells his Academy students, "with
not only what the Ancients have done, but endeavour to learn from
their works what they *would* have done. We shall, therefore, become
Artists, not mere Copyists; we shall avoid servile imitation and, what
is equally dangerous, improper application."[1] It is the familiar cry of
the "Man of Taste" calling his disciples' attention to "principles," but,
as Soane uses it, it comes nearer to being a victorious battle cry than
it did in the mouths of any of his contemporaries.

In so far as the Regency established a style in conformity with its
"principles" that style is the style of Soane. It is one which incorporates
the many new ideas that were in the air, but adopts none of them
exclusively. Style, in the eyes of the romantic Regency architect, was
a matter of suggesting approved associations, and the resulting pastiche
was the inevitable reflection of the varied ideas which he was trying to
express. Soane's style is also a pastiche, but one of basically architectural
forms rather than of literary ones. His friend, the influential "Man of
Taste," John Britton, headed his description of the Lincoln's Inn Fields
house, "The Unity of Architecture, Sculpture and Painting," a summary
which might aptly be applied to the whole of Regency architecture. What
particularly distinguishes Soane from his contemporaries is that he
keeps the three in proper perspective. Sculpture and painting are both
built-in features of his designs (to a limited extent, literature is as
well), but they are fitted into a framework designed by that rare being,
the man with a natural feeling for architectural form.

From this and from many other points of view Soane's own house
provides an excellent summary of the Regency style. He himself considered it in some such light and established it as the architectural
museum which it still remains. It has the further advantage of Britton's
sympathetic description which is itself one of the best products of
the Regency's architectural criticism.

The conditions under which it was built are typical of those which
governed the design of town buildings at the time. The site was a
restricted one and was gradually enlarged as Soane acquired additional
property: a factor which could not fail to affect the planning of the
building. Similar conditions obtained on the Bank site (91, 92, 97),
where Taylor's and Sampson's work formed the starting point of Soane's
developments. The Westminster Law Courts, which had to be planned
round the buttresses of Westminster Hall, and the country house at
Ealing (94), which included an existing block of buildings by Soane's
master, George Dance (the younger) are other buildings of Soane's

[1] Sir John Soane: *Royal Academy Lectures.*

in which he came up against those restrictions which are typical of the early nineteenth century, and which had a material effect on the development of a Picturesque type of planning.

For such buildings a regular exterior was the rule, and it called for a considerable degree of imagination on the part of the architect to arrange irregular interiors while preserving this external effect. Smirke's abilities in this direction were put severely to the test when he was faced with the design of a building to house both the Union Club and the College of Physicians (69) on an irregular site in Trafalgar Square. To make the various façades suggest the different characters of the rooms behind them, to sort out the two plans and at the same time to maintain a clear connection between them; these are problems which called for considerable architectural ability. The success with which they are solved is something of a tribute to the new-found art of irregular planning. So is the planning of the neighbouring National Gallery. Here Wilkins had to deal with a series of suites of rooms used for different purposes, each with its own entrance, and form them into a homogeneous whole. The handling of different levels in a building was fortunately one of Wilkins's specialities. The "Picturesque arrangement, the varied groupings and contrasts of the pedestals and podia"[1] which Leeds so much admired in the University College steps is an earlier example of his imaginative use of levels, and in the National Gallery, flights of steps, this time in the interior as well, were used to distinguish the different sections of the building. The planning of buildings, in the sense of making the most of a given interior space, was kept at a high level by the leading Regency architects, and these difficult sites show them adapting their technique to suit the increasing restrictions which the town site was placing on them.

The theory of the Picturesque was largely a means of circumventing the natural hazard. In the layout of buildings, as well as of gardens, it was adopted as a means of "improving" on existing conditions. In interiors it suggested ways of carving interesting architectural scenery out of sites which were too restricted to permit planning in the grand manner. It was this art which Soane brought to the pitch of perfection, and which is so ably interpreted by John Britton in his description of the Lincoln's Inn Fields house. Among other maxims laid down by him for the architect is the one that ". . . By a skilful arrangement of plan he will be able to form beautiful vistas, and views that unexpectedly burst upon the spectator, so as to fascinate him with delight; to give an appearance of greater extent to the building, and to produce that species of complexity which destroys all monotony. Instead of disclosing the whole beauties of the interior at once, the artist ought rather so to distribute the various divisions, as to present a succession of apartments gradually increasing in effect, to contrast them judicially and occasionally admit glimpses of remoter parts, in such a manner as shall forcibly affect the imagination." In such successions of spaces Soane was

[1] W. H. Leeds: *Illustration of the Public Buildings of London* (1838).

N

particularly at home. "That Mr. Soane has profoundly studied this part
of his art, must," in Britton's opinion, "be acknowledged by every one
who has examined either the building here illustrated, or the interior
of the Bank. In the former, the effect which he has attained, in this
respect, is almost unrivalled; from the first step to the last the visitor
is struck with some ingenious contrivance, some beautiful display,
some unexpected scene. The light and shade is so artfully arranged, to
produce the most piquant contrasts, that what has been primarily
adopted from necessity, appears to have been the result of study and
luxurious refinement. Parts thrown into shade serve to set off more
forcibly the brilliance of others; parts inevitably contracted tend to
add to the idea of expanse; recesses are employed to enshrine beautiful
works of art; windows are so disposed as to admit lengthened per-
spectives through courts and through the rooms." Further aims which
he holds up for the architect's consideration are that he shall so "contrive
the principal rooms, that each shall present a striking view when seen
from that adjoining," while it is " . . . also of importance that the
respective apartments should either relieve or contrast, or enhance the
effect of each other; that the imagination be called into play; and that
the whole offer to the eye a masterly arrangement and Picturesque
combination. . . ."

With these "principles" in mind, Britton proceeds to examine the
chief rooms in the house with an eye so appreciative of their architectural qualities that it is worth while enumerating the main points
of his tour.

In the Museum area at the back of the house he notices particularly the
variations in its height, between 9½ feet at its lowest and 36 feet at its
highest points, and the resulting series of contrasting views through the
house. In the "Cabinet" which opens off the Breakfast Room, he points
out that "an opening has been made in the floor, to admit a view into a
part of the lower gallery, or crypt; thus we may perceive that even a space
of a few feet may be so arranged as to produce a singularly striking effect."
From the Museum he passes to the "Student's Office," which, "When
viewed from above, or at the sides, seems suspended, or poised in middle
space, being detached from the main walls. In passing under it, the visitor
will not omit to notice a picturesque and pleasing view, which is obtained
across the courtyard, already noticed, and thence through the eating room
and library, to the garden of Lincoln's Inn Fields. Another, and very
dissimilar vista is next caught, through the dressing room, study etc., in
the same direction . . ."
From here, "Passing through a small vestibule or ante-passage, . . .
we enter the Picture Cabinet. . . . Looking back, we obtain a vista through
the whole Museum, the extreme extent of which, including the Gallery
itself, is sixty-six feet; although from the picturesque arrangement, and
the successive contrasts of light and shadow, the distance appears considerably more. The walls of this Gallery may be said to be treble, or to
consist of three surfaces, the outer one opening like folding shutters, leaving
a sufficient space between the two for pictures, both in the inner face of
the shutter, and on the wall itself. By this original and exceedingly ingenious

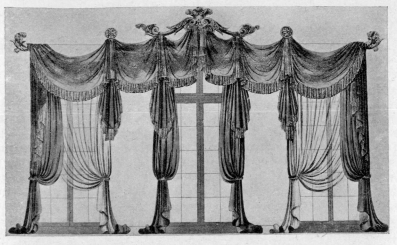

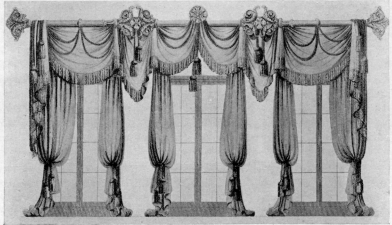

98, 99 Drawing-room Window Curtains

100 Curtains for a Gothic Room

From "The Cabinet-maker and Upholsterer's Guide," by George Smith (1826)

THE "TASTE" OF THE INTERIOR DECORATOR

101　The Main Entrance

102　The Centre Block.　*Sir John Rennie, Architect*

THE STONEHOUSE VICTUALLING YARD (1826–35)

103, 104 Villas in the Greek Style at Cheltenham. *J. B. Papworth, Architect*

105   A Sofa which gives an individual interpretation of Greek Forms

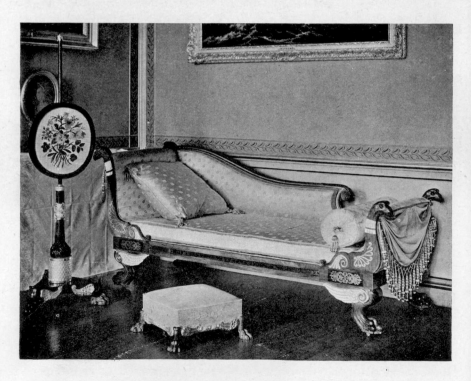

106   A Sofa, Firescreen and Footstool in the "Greek" Taste
ASPECTS OF REGENCY FURNITURE

contrivance, a small cabinet is rendered capable of containing as many pictures as a room three times the size."

"Returning to the Museum the stranger is conducted through the dressing room and small study to the eating room. The window in the dressing room commands a bird's eye view of the various architectural fragments etc. in the Court. . . ."

"We may safely assert" he states, "that nowhere within a similar extent does there exist such a succession of varied and beautiful architectural scenery, so many striking points of view, so many fascinating combinations and contrasts—so much originality, invention, contrivance, convenience and taste."

Then the Breakfast Room—

"This small and beautiful apartment is certainly not one of the least interesting in the house, whether we consider its admirable arrangements and construction, or the novelty and taste with which it is fitted up. Although its dimensions do not exceed eighteen feet by eleven, and although there are no fewer than seven doors, the disposition of the various parts is so harmonious and symmetrical, but there is no confusion or crowding, on the contrary, comfort seems to have been studied full as much as ornament. The ceiling is formed by a flattened dome perforated by a lanthorn in the centre, and by four circles in the spandrels, to the North and South of which are arched roof-windows rising above the ceiling. These throw a vertical light on the side walls, so as to produce a very beautiful effect, and to show the architectural drawings that adorn them to the utmost advantage. We have here a very happy example of the manner in which windows of this description may be introduced into sitting rooms where there are side windows also. Opposite the fireplace is a window opening to the Court, the centre compartment of which is formed by a large sheet of plate glass. Some of the doors are panelled with mirrors, which seem to give the appearance of greater extent and these being opened the museum is seen through other doors glazed with stained glass; by which views are obtained into that apartment without any inconvenience or draught of air; while, on the other hand, the objection to which doors of this description are liable, is obviated by having an inner door."

Finally he returns to the Museum, from the parapet of which ". . . various views of unusual combination and effect are obtained, both of the subterranean recess below, the gallery and dome above, and of vistas eastward towards the picture cabinet."

Such was the architectural framework on which Soane built up his individual style. Historical precedents and particularly those of the "Ancients," reflecting as they did the purity of "first principles," suggested decorative forms for rounding off the design, such as the Greek "scorings" which were not unjustifiably condemned by his critics, or the sarcophagus which gave the appropriate flavour to Desenfans' Mausoleum at Dulwich. But the whole is related to the framework of his architectural "principles."

As a step towards the "ultimate perfection" of the house which Busby saw just around the corner, Soane's style did, however, have its limitations. For one thing it was a monumental style, which treated the House as an abstract composition subject to the same laws of design

as a Bank or a Government Office building. The very real progress
which architects were making in remodelling the house to fit in with
its landscape seems to have obtained little sympathy from Soane. In
fact his buildings in this sense run counter to the whole spirit of Regency
architecture. While the typical Regency house was turning outwards

INTERIOR OF THE MAUSOLEUM, DULWICH
From Soane's *Designs for Public and Private Buildings* (1828).

and opening itself up to the surrounding landscape, Soane's buildings
turn in on themselves. His is always an architectural scene created
within four walls. To the outside world his buildings present only
academic façades. Inside they are fascinating adventures in space. But,
within his confining walls, Soane appreciated to the full that fact which
only the rarest architectural minds have realised, namely that architecture is the art, not so much of building in space, as of building space.

It was perhaps his academic background which prevented him from
appreciating the efforts of his contemporaries to build space outwards
from the house as well as inside its walls. The landscape garden, and

all that went with it, was too much of a fashion to impress Soane with its architectural possibilities. He was unstinted in his praise of the landscape garden, as a garden. He failed to see that it might have a wider architectural meaning. It is a regrettable fact that the architects who were bringing a new idea of spatiality into architecture by way of the principles of gardening were not men of outstanding architectural ability. Nash himself, in the long run, does not rise above the commonplace. His feeling for planning was highly developed both in the interior arrangement of buildings and in the wider field of relating them to their surroundings and to each other, but his plans tend to be imagined only in two dimensions, and the design of his individual buildings suffers from the slap-dash eclecticism common to architects who subscribed unthinkingly to current views of taste. In the same way significant adventures in building with space, as represented by the freely planned building designed with an eye to its surroundings, are, in the work of his contemporaries, generally disguised by the trappings of fashionable "style." Had Soane managed to pierce this disguise and bring the ideas it concealed into line with his own he might have established a style that was made to last. As it was he was content to ridicule the whole tribe of fashionable architects, landscape gardeners and "decorators" from behind the security of his own four-square façades.

Soane was in this sense one of the first of the Academicians, a self-styled escapist from the unwelcome "trend of the times." There was certainly much in them for the well-developed academic mind to deplore, but there was also much potential good in them that he over-looked. And in taking up the attitude he did Soane lost the sympathy of his contemporaries. They in turn misjudged him: so that among his many brilliant pupils there is not one who assimilated the architectural significance of his work. Soane's "principles" died with him, and with them went the hope that architecture might continue to pursue recognisable aesthetic ideals.

The Regency itself by no means lacked such ideals. If anything it had too many of them. The landscape gardeners, with their special form of "Picturesque" spatiality, the architect-engineers with their "sculpturesque" feeling for form, the "Arbiters of Taste" themselves, who sorted out the literary associations of the "Styles": all were approaching from different angles towards a true "Unity of architecture, sculpture and painting." The foundations of a style were there, but the style itself never materialised as a homogeneous structure. Instead there arose a diverting but, from the architect's point of view, an entirely inconsequential series of façades in different styles. The "trend of the times" which Soane deplored, and which the "Man of Taste" strove to direct into fruitful architectural channels, is towards a rugged individualism in style, as in the social background which made such an attitude inevitable.

The "Man of Taste" was doing his best to prevent this drift towards a promiscuous indulgence in "Style," but his pleas for restraint sound faint beside the clamour of a middle class investing in "art" as the outward and visible sign of their prosperity. The "collections" of the Dilettanti were having their brief day in private galleries, but they were already on their way to the museums where the "true taste" of the Regency was destined to end. What survived was the bric-à-brac taste of a public whose eye for getting its moneys-worth in decoration was to be admirably caught by Disraeli in his descriptions of the early Victorian interior. J. B. Papworth, whose carefree ranging over the plastic arts is commemorated in his adoption of the middle name of "Buonarotti," was among the architects who were laying the foundations for this taste during the Regency. His correspondence with his client James Morrison shows Papworth in the new role of the architect, acting in this case as an intermediary between that "Napoleon of Shop-Keepers" and the rising trades of furniture-dealing and interior decoration.

"If you should see anything," writes Morrison, "Clocks and old China at Paris which you should approve for us, I should be obliged to your getting M.P. . . . to purchase it, or point out to him, so that we may advise him to buy it after your return. The dealers from London are now purchasing freely old carved frames and clocks of the age of Louis XV. . . . I am very anxious about Turner. If I get very good things I shall become attach'd to the Arts; if otherwise, I shall desert them for another hobby. I have spent £1200, including China etc. last year . . . I am told you gave no positive order for a frame for 'Christ healing the sick.' Pray do it when you are passing Cribb's." On another occasion: "Choose a paper for the library at Morants', the patterns and colours I must say nothing about, I am so bad a judge of these things. . . . A frame for Mrs. Siddon's print." "I was too late again for Prout. I could not go in time, and if I had I should rather have had your judgment than mine. Why won't you look for me? Are you watching the appearance of any new engraving to lay hold of a very fine copy for me?"[1]

To guide his client in the choice of such embellishments for his house was, however, a task for which few architects had either the time or the inclination, and the interior decorator was not behindhand in stepping into the breach. He arrives in a blaze of tasteful glory in the person of Maria Edgworth's Mr. Soho. In describing the transformation of Lady Colambre's rooms for her ball, that worthy can most effectively be allowed to speak for himself. Protracted as it is, his is the last word in the assortment of styles which were drawn on for embellishing the Regency house.

"You fill up your angles here with *encoinieres*," he directs, ". . . round your walls with the *Turkish tent drapery*—a fancy of my own—in apricot cloth, or crimson velvet, suppose, or *en flute*, in crimson satin draperies, fanned and riched with gold fringes, *en suite*—intermediate spaces,

---

[1] "John B. Papworth, Architect to the King of Wurtemburg." By Wyatt Papworth (1879).

108   A Bookcase, with drapery hangings on the wall behind

107   A Mirror, placed to reflect a picturesque view

FEATURES OF THE REGENCY INTERIOR

109　A monumental version of the Greek in Regent's Park, London:
No. 1, Gloucester Gate. *J. J. Scoles, Architect*

110　Greek Trimmings applied to a Villa on the Promenade, Cheltenham

111   Holwood, Kent (1825).   *Decimus Burton, Architect*

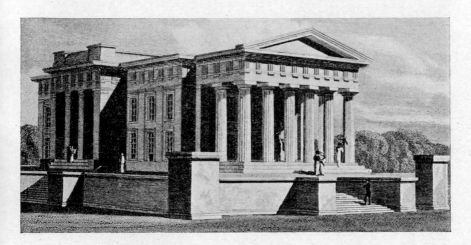

112   Grange Park, Hampshire (*c.* 1810).   *William Wilkins, Architect*

113   House in Regent's Park, London (1822).   *Decimus Burton, Architect*

"GRECIAN" HOUSE DESIGN

114 Urban Design in the Georgian Tradition: Park Crescent, Regent's Park (1823–5). *John Nash, Architect*

115 "Rus in Urbe": a group of Villas on Herne Hill

Both illustrations from Ackermann's "Repository . . ."

Apollo's heads with gold rays—and here ma'am, you place four *chancelieres*, with chimeras at the corners, covered with blue silk and silver fringe, elegantly fanciful—with my STATIRA CANOPY here—light blue silk draperies—aerial tint, with silver balls—and for the seats here, the SERAGLIO OTTOMANS, superfine scarlet—your paws—griffin—golden—and golden tripods, here, with antique cranes—and oriental alabaster tables here and there—quite appropriate, your La'ship feels.

"And let me reflect. For the next apartment, it strikes me—as your La'ship don't value expense—the *Alhambra hangings*—my own thought entirely. . . . So see Ma'am (unrolling them)—scagliogla Porphyry columns supporting the grand dome—entablature, silvered and decorated with imitative bronze ornaments: under the entablature, a *valance in pelmets*, of puffed scarlet silk, would have an unparalleled grand effect, seen through the arches—with the TREBISOND TRELLICE PAPER, would make a *tout ensemble*, novel beyond compare. On that Trebisond trellice paper, I confess, ladies, I do figure myself.

"Then, for the little room, I recommend turning it temporarily into a Chinese Pagoda, with this *Chinese Pagoda paper*, with the *porcelain border*, and josses, and jars, and beakers, to match; and I can venture to promise one vase of pre-eminent size and beauty. Oh indubitably! If your La'ship prefers it, you can have the Egyptian *hieroglyphic paper*, with the *ibis border* to match: the only objection is, one sees it every-where,—quite antediluvian—gone to the hotels even; but, to be sure, if your La'ship has a fancy; at all events, I humbly recommend, what her Grace of Torcaster longs to patronise, my MOON CURTAINS, with candlelight draperies. A *demi-saison* elegance this—I hit off yesterday—and—true, your La'ship's quite correct—out of the common completely. And, of course, you'd have the *sphynx candelabras*, and the phoenix argadns—O! nothing else lights now, ma'am!"[1]

A taste which can only appeal to fashion is clearly in the last archi-tectural ditch. That the Regency managed to hold out as it did in such a position is at least some tribute to the "Man of Taste" and his principles. In this final phase of keeping the hordes of a philistine society at bay, Georgian "sensibility" was doing its last and some of its noblest work. It was inevitably coarsened a little, but about the Sphinxes, the Root-work and the SERAGLIO OTTOMANS there still hovers the ghost of sensitive Georgian craftsmanship. The architect and the decorator might cull his motives from India, China or from the filigree depths of his own imagination, but he still managed to impress them with the mark of a discriminating sense of form.

To pillage motives from all available sources may be the sign of a lack of individual imagination. To do so successfully is certainly the test of a designer's sensibility, and as such Regency architects considered it. To catalogue characteristic "features" and to explore "sources of inspiration" for their decorative forms would be a monumental task in the case of this architecture which drew on such varied ones. It is

[1] Maria Edgworth: *The Absentee*.

also irrelevant in a style whose individuality shows through its orna-
mentation to the extent that the Regency's does. Their perorations on
taste should not be allowed to blind us to the fact that this is the way
in which Regency architects would have liked us to consider their
designs: and it may rest as a final justification of them that we are able to
recognise this intention.

116   A Terrace in Mecklenburg Square, Bloomsbury (1812).
Joseph Kay, Architect

117   Porches emphasise individual
houses in the Paragon, Clifton

118   29, Dover Street, London: once
the office of John Nash
John Nash, Architect (1810)

TYPES OF TOWN HOUSE

119 Euston Square, London. A Terrace on the Bedford Estate, laid out by the builder Thomas Cubitt

V

Town and Countryside

THE questions of taste with which the Regency was most occupied
were those concerned with the landscape and of the architecture which
formed a part of it. In fact it might be said that taste was initially a
country product. Its manifestations appeared on the country estate
long before they reached the town. The former was at least its particular
province during the eighteenth century. Architects and their patrons
thought of taste in terms of the country house, while the town was more
often than not left at the mercy of the speculator and the builder. This,
however, can no longer be said of the Regency. The attention he gave to
"improving" his country property did not prevent the landowner from
discovering the town and from bringing his taste to bear on its appearance. And, in doing so, he evolved an idea of town architecture which
was highly individual and appropriate, one which produced a fitting
frame for his own culture and which is by no means without significance
for our own times.

The English town had always remained close to nature. Its conscious
planning had been something of an elaboration of the village, whose
layout is freely adapted to the contours of the countryside. Those
external considerations of military strategy and the geometrical frenzy
of cultured princes which together produced the much-admired
continental "town-plans," these had played negligible parts in the
making of the English town. Such a limited feeling for order and
architectural layout as appeared in it came from more domestic sources,
among them the monastic courtyard and the quadrangle of the university town. A town laid out as a town hardly existed until eighteenth-
century Bath. And this in spite of its geometrical framework, is a town
whose plan interprets many of the characteristics of the village and the
university quadrangle in terms of a sophisticated taste. Regency
architects did not overlook this remarkable precedent (Nash's Regents
Park layout owes a great deal to the circuses and crescents of Bath),
but they had much of their own to add to the forms it established.

Theirs was above all an effort to break down the barrier between
town and countryside, and a wider application of the principles of
taste to this end. Kent, who "leaped the fence and saw that all nature
was a garden," was in the Regency followed by Nash, who leaped the
outer circle of town houses and discovered that the whole town could
be a landscape. It was perhaps less of an athletic achievement than
Kent's, because others had already partly demolished the barrier. The

P

aristocrat who came to town bringing his taste with him, had ridden
rough-shod over it, while his city-bred imitator had bridged it from
the other side when he emulated a "rural" character in his town house.
It was from this two-way traffic that there resulted the architectural
congestion (115), which is appropriately seen on the main roads leading
out of London, on the Wandsworth Road and the Brixton Road particularly, where terraces and villas in all shades of conformity with the
precepts of "Taste" commemorate this demolition of the fence that Nash
leaped. Cruikshank's cartoon of Regency "ribbon development" shows
the first steps in this "march of bricks and mortar." Its final effort is
recorded with equal distaste by Coleman, who contemplates the scene:

> Stretching round England's chief Emporium far,
> No rage for Building quench'd by raging War,
> What would-be villas, ranged in dapper pride,
> Usurp the fields, and choke the highway side!
> Peace to each swain, who rural rapture owns,
> As soon as past a toll, or off the stones.[1]

Loudon for one had already subscribed to the depressing philosophy
which is implied in the idea that "the very purpose for which we engage
in commerce is that we may one day be enabled to retire to the country."[2]

But while Brixton was the furthest that many Londoners got in their
pursuit of the pleasures of "retirement," those who had indulged more
successfully in commerce were able to invade the precincts of the
country estate itself with their villas and *Cottages Ornées*. During
the Regency period the break-up of the country estates had already
begun, and the landscaped estate was being split up into plots for these
"country cottages" designed according to the townsman's second-hand
idea of landscaped architecture. Cobbett's diatribes against Pitt's paper
money are symbolical of the countryman's indignation at the defeat of
his ideals by the new industrial economy. "All this comes o' paper
money, Master Hawthorn," echoes the Squire in *Melincourt* "(and
all the while he was nailing up a window or two every year, and his
horses were going one way, and his dogs another, and his old servants
were zent away one by one)": and in the same strain Master Hawthorn
abuses the ancestors of "stockbrokers Tudor" architecture which were
invading the estate. For "every now and then a queer zort o' chap
dropped out o' the sky like—a vundholder he called un—and brought
a bit of ground vor a handful o' paper, and built a cottage horny as
they call it—there be one there on the hillside—and had nothing to do
wi' the country people nor the country people wi' he: nothing in the
world to do, as could zee, but to eat and drink, and make little bits
o' shrubberies, o' quashies, and brutuses, and zalies, and filigrees, and
ruddydunderums, instead o' the oak plantations the old landlords used
to plant; and the Squire could never abide the sight o' one o' they
gimcrack boxes. . . ."[3]

---

[1] Coleman's *Eccentricities*.   [2] *Country Residences*.   [3] Peacock: *Melincourt*.

London going out of Town — or — The March of Bricks & mortar.

REGENCY "RIBBON DEVELOPMENT"
From a cartoon by Cruikshank

In the *cottage ornée* the fundholder had taken a well-thumbed leaf out of the "Man of Taste's" book. Marie Antoinette's pursuit of "retirement" in an expurgated edition of a dairy had set the pace for these, as Malton appropriately describes them ". . . abodes suitable to receive swollen man . . . when he shrinks into himself again."[1] With the help of the lending library, the taste for the Picturesque cottage had been brought full circle from the "ennui" of the empress to the tiredness of the business man.

The break-up of the country estate was largely a matter of economic necessity. It was also to a certain extent a matter of choice. The nomadic instincts incited by such Picturesque Tours as Dr. Syntax's and the development of a definite town culture were among the many inducements which led the country landowner to migrate to a more urban setting. For in spite of all their efforts, the landscape gardeners did not altogether succeed in making the country estate appear a more attractive background for the "Man of Taste" than the town or the untouched countryside. It was perhaps a case of "wishful thinking" that architects like Malton should have considered such scenes as being preferable to the country estate. It is nevertheless a sign of the times that he should be able to say without a qualm that "walking in a stately park always makes me melancholy"[2] and that he should consider the "flight . . ." of its owner "to the watering-place, to the villa, to the humble cottage" to be a manifestation of "correct Taste." Malton even tries to make architectural capital of this movement by suggesting that a series of houses in different situations is a desirable alternative to the isolated country estate. These houses would "differ from each other . . . as style and magnitude and situation, society, or partial pleasure might be the cause of their erection. . . . A villa might," he considers, "be built in several distinct neighbourhoods, or on each different estate, should they lay widely asunder; a hunting box at one place, a shooting box at another; with a cottage or other small tenement for the amusement of angling; as also dwellings on the sea shore for marine advantages."[3]

At least one important result of this migratory movement was that the watering place and the seaside town came to have their fair share of the "Man of Taste's" attentions, and in turn to derive recognisable qualities from the layout of the country estate. For in the wake of the "Man of Taste" there followed the principles of layout and the Picturesque theories which had enjoyed their first successes in the layout of the landscape garden. The same principles, applied to the design of town housing estates, were responsible for some of the most concrete achievements of Regency architects. Already, on his own estate, the "Man of Taste" had found himself indulging in a modest form of town-planning as he followed his bent for Picturesque layout. Repton's preoccupation with the boundaries of a gentleman's estate has already been mentioned, and considered from this point of view,

[1] James Malton: *Designs for Villas* (1802).   [2] Ibid.   [3] Ibid.

121   Brunswick Terrace, Hove

122   Lansdowne Place, Worthing

ESTATE DEVELOPMENT IN SEASIDE TOWNS

120 A characteristic Regency Town Layout with houses overlooking a planted space: The West Mall, Clifton, Bristol

it is seen to be much more than the mere matter of snobbishness it appears on first sight. If a village belonged to the estate it was clearly in the best interests of the Picturesque "improver" that it should be included in the composition and that its design should in this way make some contribution to the finished picture. The earlier landscapists had moved whole villages, rather than blemish the "natural" landscape with such evidence of its contemporary purpose. The village of Milton Abbas, rebuilt, as it was, in a tree-rimmed pit in the landscape, remains as a visible evidence of this phase of "town-planning" the landscape. Characteristic of the different outlook adopted by Regency architects are Nash's hamlet of Picturesque cottages at Blaise Castle (89, 90) and the group of cottages, designed to be seen from the grounds of Fonthill, which appropriately reflected the architecture of Ludlow Castle.

The shortage of labourers' cottages and the general "housing problem" which followed the spread of the Speenhamland system of allowances gave the landlords ample opportunity for experiments in laying out Picturesque housing estates. Dearn's design for a Gothic lodge entrance to Bayham Abbey (22), consisting of a series of "flats," is an extreme case of the pressing of this rural housing shortage into the service of the Picturesque. Such ideas may not have been of any particular significance as precedents for the design of town houses. They at least accustomed architects to think of cottages and other incidental buildings as forming part of an "estate" which was of uniform Picturesque appearance throughout. They were also responsible for bringing Picturesque layout into the light of day and prepared the way for adapting it to the planning of housing estates. For when, in such cases as the Bayham entrance, the Picturesque spread beyond the actual confines of the garden, its products were made visible not only to the cultivated amateur, who had become accustomed to seeing them from the rides in his Park, but to the admiring public who could now contemplate them from the high road. Such is literally the case with the incidental buildings on the Redleaf estate at Penshurst. An ornamental gardener's cottage, which Loudon quotes in his *Encyclopedia* as an admirable example of Rustic design, stands near the road, but obliquely facing it and apparently belonging to the garden layout. On the opposite side of the road, however, are a pair of cottages, which have nothing to do with the garden layout but are nevertheless designed in the Picturesque half-timbered style. Inscribed as they are, with the date 1824, they must be among the first examples of the spread of the "Elizabethan" revival beyond the boundary of the Picturesque garden. At the end of the Regency Period designs in the "Rustic" style, which was essentially the counterpart of the "gone-to-earth" school of the landscape gardeners, are even found so far afield as in a fashionable watering-place. For at Beulah Spa, Norwood, Decimus Burton designed a series of buildings which are described by the *Mirror* of 1832 as being ". . . in the best taste of ornate rusticity, with the characteristic varieties of gable, and dripstone, portico, bay-window and embellished chimney."

Q

The breaking down of the barriers between town and countryside was in fact being paralleled by the disappearance of the boundary to the country estate. The latter let loose the principles of Picturesque design into the open countryside. The former opened the way for the adaptation of landscape principles to the layout of the town itself.

The garden had first seen the shaping of scenery in conformity with current ideals of natural beauty. The Regency town witnessed corresponding attempts to treat housing "estates" in the same way. In the garden at Redleaf a remarkable outcrop of sandstone rock had been used as a romantic feature of the layout, with walks planned through it and the house sited so as to exploit a Picturesque view of it. In the neighbouring town of Tunbridge Wells outcrops of the same stone suggested an attempt to plan a whole town around this natural feature. This countryside was well calculated to stimulate the imagination of the Picturesque connoisseur. Mrs. Montague, for example, describes a scene in which Pitt gave an alfresco recital on his french horn, after which the party dispersed to admire views ". . . some wild as Salvator Rosa, others placid, and with the setting sun, worthy of Claude Lorrain."[1] Mrs. Carter bears her friend out in defining the scenery as being "the most perfectly romantic I had ever seen, except in the descriptions of poets, or the paintings of Salvator Rosa. . . . All was wild, spontaneous beauty, and what Mr. Mason finely calls 'The lone majesty of untamed nature'."

The existence of so much Sublimity in the immediate neighbourhood of a chalybeate spring and within accessible distance of London were considerations which led to interesting developments in the town in the late eighteenth century. Visits to the "High Rocks" were soon found to provide insufficient stimulus for sublime imaginings and the visitors to "The Wells" set about bringing Salvator Rosa nearer home by building houses among the rocks on the common. The Master of Ceremonies, Paul Amsinck, records the migration of what had hitherto remained a seasonal colony of visitors to these new sites, in some cases literally taking their houses with them: one such removal being recorded in which the house was "preceded by a band of music and a jovial company drinking success to the purchaser."[2] A sufficient number of these houses, built actually on the rocks and "erected," according to Amsinck, "apparently without a plan or semblance of regularity," remain to show the effect of this embryo effort at the landscaped town.

Not far away Decimus Burton's Calverley Estate shows the way in which Regency architects finally reduced the idea to a practical form of "Estate Development." The series of houses overlooking a landscaped park and served by a shopping centre (afterwards converted into a terrace of houses) (125), a market (123), and a tradesmen's quarter, represents their standard compromise between the demands of Picturesque "amenity" and economic necessity. For the landscaped town after the manner of the early Tunbridge Wells was neither a practical

[1] Mrs. Montague: *Letters* (1809).   [2] Paul Amsinck: *Tunbridge Wells* (1805).

123 The Market (later Town Hall)   124 A House with Shops below

125 Calverley Crescent. *Decimus Burton, Architect*

THE CALVERLEY ESTATE, TUNBRIDGE WELLS

126 Brunswick Square, North Side: speculative houses on the Foundling Estate, Bloomsbury

127 Part of the Bedford Estate, Bloomsbury. Russell Square (*left*) was laid out by Humphry Repton

economic proposition at a time when London alone was catering for a population which increased from 88,000 in 1801 to 1,500,000 in 1831; nor could its absence of "a semblance of regularity" satisfy architects whose essays in the Picturesque always departed from a semblance of Georgian order (114). Bringing the country into the town in general involved some form of compromise with existing ideas of an ordered community. The Georgian tradition was an extremely rigid one so far as the town house was concerned and the separation of houses into different "rates" according to their superficial area had crystallised their design into what must be the most extreme form of "standardisation" known in the history of English architecture. In their layout there did, however, persist a sufficient reflection of the forms of village layout and the monastic plan to suggest a point of departure for Regency architects.

This was particularly so in the case of the London squares. The idea may have been partly a foreign one, derived as it was from Inigo Jones's layout of Covent Garden in imitation of a fashionable continental "piazza." The squares which followed it in the eighteenth century nevertheless acquired something of a characteristic native air. The very acts under which many of them were laid out hint at a monastic sense of community. The Regency development of Brunswick (126) and Mecklenburg Squares (116) round the Foundling Hospital still placed many obligations on the tenants in the form of contributions to the upkeep of the neighbourhood. The layout of the central garden, and its maintenance particularly, were the concern of a board of Commissioners representing the residents in the squares and the governors of the Foundling Hospital. Rates "up to one shilling in the pound" were levied on the residents for this purpose. This idea of laying out a central garden in a residential square to be used by the residents and maintained by them is a democratic feature of Georgian planning which is very far removed from the paved promenade of the continental piazza. More than that it provided a point of departure for architects developing the idea of the "garden city."

James Burton, when he laid out his housing estate round Bloomsbury Square in the early nineteenth century, planned it in the form of regular blocks of houses forming open squares and enclosed gardens, with Repton making his contribution to the layout in the form of a project for the planting of Russell Square (127). But here, as on most of the occasions on which he was consulted in the layout of squares, Repton himself had little of value to contribute to the idea of the landscaped housing estate. His eye for architecture as an element in the landscape was reliable enough when it was free to rove in the country park. It was less so when confined within the framework of city streets. In the case of Russell Square, the levelling of the site before he was consulted admittedly deprived him of those natural undulations which were the foundations on which he built his park layouts. All the same, more might have been expected of him than the mere encirclement of the garden by a "belt" of trees and shrubs; a feature which he carefully avoided in the planting of parks. The idea that the planting of a square should be considered in relation to the surrounding architecture, not obscuring it but making a Picturesque composition of the whole, was one which simply does not seem to have occurred to him. It was left for others, and particularly for his former collaborator, John Nash, to develop the Regency "garden city" in conformity with more architectural principles.

The Regency ideal of transplanting the countryside in the town raised problems both for the landscape gardener and for the architect. The two might be solved by one man, as they were by J. B. Papworth, who gave evidence of his prowess in both capacities when he laid out the Cheltenham estates. Alternatively, members of the two professions might work in collaboration, as they did in the syndicate composed of Nash, the young Reptons and the former head gardener at Kew, William Townsend Aiton. The latter's expert hand can be detected in the layout of St. James's Park, Regent's Park and the Brighton Pavilion Garden. By whatever means it might be brought about, the builder's idea of the Picturesque had to be reconciled with the planter's view of it before any positive results could be expected in town planning. To ignore the builder, as Repton did, ruled out the possibility of obtaining any such results. For ideas of Picturesque design were now changing the appearance of the city street scarcely less than they had affected the appearance of the country house, and "escape from Georgian plainness" was recognised by at least one commentator on the town house as being a necessary counterpart to the emulation of *rus in urbe*.

The effect of Picturesque principles on town architecture was perhaps less widespread. For while the country labourer might be considered as a Picturesque object and his home a subject to be treated accordingly, his city counterpart could not be viewed in any such light, and his home remained outside the frame of the landscaped town. Southey, who judged industrial civilisation by the lack of picturesqueness in its cottages, perhaps represents the furthest point reached by commentators on the appearance of the embryo slum: and he was summarily dealt with by Macaulay, for thus making ". . . the Picturesque the test of political good" . . . Rose-bushes and poor-rates, rather than steamengines and independence. Mortality and cottages with weather-stains, rather than health and long life with edifices which time cannot mellow":[1] on these distorted issues the apostles of the new age could hold only one opinion. "Steam-engines and independence" won the day. If "health and long life" failed to follow it was still no concern of the architect. But, although large areas of the town were excluded from its benefits, the effect of Picturesque theory on the appearance of towns was a marked one.

Old John Burton may not have been as familiar with fashionable ideas as his son Decimus proved himself to be, but even he avoided the absolutely regular façade of street houses, and in Bedford Place used subtle indentations in the façades as a means of escaping from the other-

[1] Macaulay: *Literary Essays.*

wise "Georgian plainness" of his street. Cubitt, who carried on his sequence of squares, fell more obviously into line with Picturesque tendencies and introduced pilastered features in the Adam manner to close the vistas down the sides of Gordon Square. In Tavistock Square similar forms are developed to form one of those sophisticated "terraces" which were the ultimate outcome of applying Picturesque ideas to the design of housing estates. Cubitt, as a successful builder who moved with the times, is as good a guide to follow as any in this development away from the standardised Georgian house, and his break away from the tradition by making a limited use of stucco features in the Bedford Estate squares was later elaborated into those all-stucco fronts of Belgrave Square which set the scale for Victorian design.

In Cubitt's buildings the "terrace" form is clearly seen for what it was, namely another aspect of the playing of Picturesque ideas into the hands of a middle class bent on expressing their aspirations in architectural terms. The stylised "terrace" of houses, with their appearance of forming a single palatial building, was not only a more Picturesque object than the standard house in a uniform row. It was also more in harmony with the aim of "keeping up appearances." The same idea was responsible for that other significant departure from the uniform street, the semi-detached house. "Houses built in couples," decides Thompson, "are not only attended with less expense than when detached, but they are calculated to present an appearance of consequence which singly they might not possess."[1] By way of such considerations a new theatrical quality appeared in the design of housing estates which became an essential element in the landscaped town. The fine architectural quality which eighteenth-century builders had obtained by way of a repetition of uniform houses was disregarded in the more advanced examples of Regency planning. It is still found in the quarters of those "lower orders" in the social scale which were considered to be altogether beyond the pale of the Picturesque. The "fourth" and "fifth" rate houses classified by the London Building Act of 1774 are from this point of view perhaps more worthy architecturally than their more Picturesque counterparts of the first three "rates." But from the wider, town-planning point of view, the cramping of them into confined streets ignored the contribution which landscape gardening was making to the layout of towns. The Regency town was in this sense very limited in its scope. The Picturesque was as much a social concept as an aesthetic one and its effects on town planning were limited accordingly. To extend the benefits of landscape planning to the housing of the "lower orders," even had architects considered it to be part of their job, would have involved an understanding of economic factors which lay beyond the scope of most "Men of Taste."

There is, however, a unique case of an industrial town being designed throughout to include the "amenities" of the landscape. This was in the "Villages of Union and Co-operation" projected by Robert Owen in

[1] *Retreats.*

his *New View of Society*. Owen, as manager of the New Lanark Mills,
had acquired his views on town-planning in a practical school. By
sheer economic foresight he had been able to turn a dingy industrial
colony, redolent of the horrors of early nineteenth-century capitalism,
into a model community, well kept and flourishing economically to the
tune of £60,000 profit under the first ten years of his managership, and
equipped with schools, savings bank, co-operative stores and a
"community centre."

Owen's achievement at New Lanark was known all over Europe, and
between 1814 and 1824 this remote Scottish village had an average of
some 2,000 admiring visitors a year, among them the Grand Duke
Nicholas of Russia, who offered to form a model province under Owen's
managership composed of 2,000,000 of the "surplus" population of
the British Isles. Had the Grand Duke's project taken shape it would
no doubt have borne considerable resemblance to the "Villages of
Union and Co-operation," those visions of a working-class garden city
which Peacock describes adequately enough when he caricatures
Robert Owen in the guise of "Mr. Toogood, the co-operationist, who
will have neither fighting nor praying; but wants to parcel out the world
into squares like a chess-board, with a community on each, raising
everything for one another, with a great steam-engine to serve them in
common for tailor and hosier, kitchen and cook."[1] Peacock is justifiably
sceptical of the actual appearance of Owen's chess-board communities,
and his readers must have agreed that they were hopelessly unpicturesque. But this by no means impairs their architectural value, which
lies in Robert Owen's being one of the first to realise that the landscaped
city could only be a practical possibility if some account were taken of
wider social considerations.

He saw that the ideal of *rus in urbe* must remain confined to luxury
housing estates unless it could be reconciled with a wider economic
plan. The one he suggested involved a programme of "State Works"
and that ownership of land by the community which was an essential
preliminary to the "Garden City" planning which has realised some of
the Regency architects' ambitions in our own time: (and which would
have been more successful had the Regency town been studied in a
spirit of proper humility). Architecturally, Owen had to make the departure from tradition which is implied in housing his communities in
blocks of "flats." This was a move which would have helped Regency
architects enormously, had they been able to appreciate its value in
freeing a larger ground area for landscape layout. Robert Owen had the
Scottish precedent to go on: for in the Scottish cities the flat was a
traditional form of housing; but Regency London saw only such random
experiments in flat building as the conversion of York House by Henry
Holland into the "Albany" apartments. Holland, however, made the
most of the flat as an individual architectural form, and his apartments
have straightforward and well-shaped plans which might have been

[1] Peacock: *Crotchet Castle*.

130 Donnington Hall, Leicestershire. An early design by William Wilkins
in the "Castellated Style"

131 The Royal Lodge, Windsor. Originally designed by Nash; altered by Wyatt
("*Country Life*" *Photograph*)

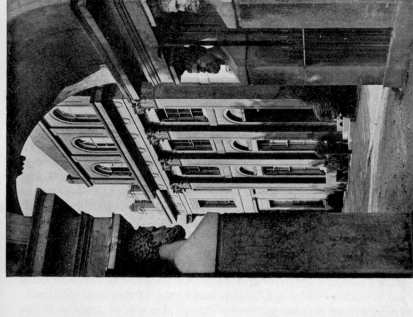

129   The Entrance to Park Crescent, Worthing

PICTURESQUE APPROACHES TO REGENCY TERRACES

128   The Entrance to Chester Terrace, Regent's Park (1825)
John Nash, Architect

studied with advantage by the "pioneers" of flat building later in the century. Macaulay gives them a good testimonial when he describes his flat in the Albany as "a very comfortable suite of chambers . . ." consisting of "an Entrance Hall, two Sitting-rooms, a Bedroom, a Kitchen, Cellars and two rooms for servants, all for ninety guineas a year. . . ."[1] Considering that this was, as Macaulay says "in a situation which the younger son of a Duke need not be ashamed of," it is surprising that an architecture so eminently governed by speculation as the Regency's, should have failed to carry the idea any further. As it was, building enterprise was limited to cramming the requisite number of houses on to a given site and introducing as much landscape planting as could be provided economically for the higher "rates" of houses.

It was an accepted limitation of house-building in the Regency towns that it was almost entirely in the hands of speculative builders, by whom landscape planting and Picturesque features were considered as "amenities," to be grafted on to existing patterns as cheaply as possible. Builders like Burton and Cubitt did their job conscientiously and in some cases seem to have had sufficient respect for "correct taste," as a contributor to letting value, to consult architects over their designs. The common run of builders, however, either stuck to such admirable patterns as those in Nicholson's *Dictionary*, or, departing from this increasingly unfashionable standard, they produced versions of contemporary "Taste" as doubtful as that of the public for which it was provided.

The meeting-ground of town and countryside where ribbon-development already held sway, acquired its full complement of houses reflecting the various facets of taste indiscriminately. Such features are noted as accompaniments to the invasion of the countryside by the "would-be-Villas" of the would-be "Man of Taste":

> Where the prig Architect, with "style" in view,
> Has dol'd his houses forth, in two by two,
> And rear'd a Row upon the plan, no doubt,
> Of old men's jaws, with every third tooth out.
> Or where, still greater lengths of taste to go,
> He warps his tenements into a bow;
> Nails a scant canvas, propt on slight deal sticks,
> Nicknamed "Verandah," to the first-floor bricks;
> Before the whole, in one smug sequent drawn,
> Claps half a rood of turf he calls a lawn;
> Then chuckling at his lath-and-plaster bubble,
> Dubs it the Crescent—and the rents are double.[2]

Most of the features are easily recognised ones. The verandah as an echo of the Picturesque country house, the "lawn" as a contraction of its garden, and the crescent as a form giving varied views of an open prospect. The incongruity of such features on an arterial road and reproduced to a mean scale is obvious enough, but it would be easier to

---

[1] Letter to Mr. Ellis, July 12, 1841.　　　　　　　[2] Colman's *Eccentricities*.

describe them as "eccentricities" if we were less familiar with worse ones to-day. What to the Regency critic seemed a meagre "lawn" fronting the houses, is now considered a sufficiently valuable feature for the idea to have been entertained of converting the continuous strip of gardens along the Brixton Road into a boulevard: while many of the houses themselves, in spite of their second-hand reflections of "Taste," remain sufficiently near to the fine standard of the pattern books to make their destruction a matter of concern to preservation societies. In the streets of Brixton, that happy hunting-ground of the Regency caricaturist, there is a wealth of examples of really fine buildings and well-planted prospects.

The criticism which really is justified is the haphazard appearance of much of this architecture. Different ideas on the Picturesque were, in the builder's hands, destroying the sense of unity which was implicit in the Georgian town. The uniform row of houses was, for "idealogical" reasons, giving way to the individual terrace, the semi-detached house and the self-assertive villa. At the same time the design of individual houses was running the whole gamut of "styles," between the "Grecian" of the villa and the "Rustic" of those cottages embellished with "tree-trunks instead of columns" which Pocock found so incongruous in the London suburbs. Even such a unifying feature as the flat skyline was being ruled out by a return to the more individual and Picturesque form of the pitched roof.

Given control of a sufficiently large area, the architect could organise such forms and relate them to his planting so that they contributed to a satisfactory whole. But, on plots along a regular street front, Picturesque architecture came close to chaos. The builder had proved himself competent enough in handling the geometric regularity of the eighteenth-century street. Picturesque layout clearly needed the guiding hand of the architect, and it was in cases where the two managed to come to terms that the most successful Regency estates were produced. Papworth in particular was an architect who publicised the idea that the architect's touch was indispensable in stamping a building with the hall-mark of "correct taste." The same villas round London which Coleman's *Eccentricities* ascribe to the "prig architect" are referred to by Papworth as being the work of builders, and he further regrets that "the speculative builder has also superseded the artist, for the architect is there (in London) rarely called upon, unless it be to remedy the errors, or supply some of the deficiencies, as well of art as of practical science."[1] The way in which he collaborated with builders, so that the requisite degree of "Taste" could be introduced without detriment to the builder's pocket, is described in the conditions under which the *Maison Dieu* estate at Dover was laid out.

The designs were made by Papworth and conditions drawn up specifying the materials to be used, in this case stuccoed brick and slate roofing, such details as fencing ("to be stone curb and iron railings")

[1] J. B. Papworth: *Rural Residences* (1818).

132, 133   Park Village West: a romantic backwater in Regent's Park.
John Nash, Architect (1824)

134   Villas on Streatham Hill, grouped free of their access road

135   Cumberland Terrace.   Part of the scenic façade overlooking Regent's Park.   *John Nash, Architect*

drains, party walls, etc. Papworth's drawings and specification had to be followed by the builders or other lessees of the plots. "The plans and building conditions," states a final clause "are to be accurately followed . . . under forfeiture of the lease." Agreements drawn up on these lines gave Papworth, for one, every opportunity to remedy the absence of "Taste" evident in those "rule and square excrescences," as he terms them, which were springing up ". . . in the neighbourhood of London."

It was a maxim of Edmund Bartell's that "where the seeds of judgment have not been sown in the mind, no produce can be looked for when our necessities call for action" and, in conformity with it, the uncultivated mind of the Regency builder was held to be incapable of answering the "Man of Taste's" call to action. To-day we can admire the straightforward planning and subtle feeling for proportion which distinguishes his work. The true "Man of Taste" considered, as Papworth did, that it was only the architect who was capable of raising these buildings into the higher realms of taste. Hence, even if the town house remained largely in the hands of the speculative builder, it was nevertheless the architect who took the lead so far as design was concerned. Unfortunately it is difficult for us to share the Regency architect's enthusiasm for this return of the town house to the bosom of self-conscious "art." The general verdict must be that it had been much better off under the eighteenth-century builder, who may have made little profession of architectural knowledge, but who had acquired a feeling for the essentials which Regency architects came more and more to overlook. By-products of the pursuit of the Picturesque were numerous town houses and street blocks of charming and original design but, in many of them, architectural essentials are obscured by some superficial concession to a fashionable style. This is particularly so in the case of "terraces" of houses, the idea behind which was an essentially theatrical one, and which often suffer from being considered as mere façades. Nash is a particular offender in this respect. His blocks in Regent's Park (128, 135), together with those of the other architects involved, turn an agreeable enough face to the park, but there is no attempt to give their backs even the semblance of architectural regularity. It was one of the limitations of the Picturesque, as applied to the design of housing estates, that there was, as it were, no wall on which to hang the completed picture. Instead there were streets from which nothing could be seen except the back of the frame.

From this, and from many other points of view, the new approach to the design of the town house was very much bound up with the methods of laying out the landscaped estate: and it was in their layouts rather than in the design of individual buildings, that Regency architects made such a valuable advance on the eighteenth-century builder's methods.

The ideal Regency housing estate is something of a compromise between two forms of planning: between the haphazard landscape town, as represented by romantic Tunbridge Wells, and the rule-of-thumb layouts of the eighteenth-century builders. The gentleman's town house must look out over a landscape and also form a part of it in the same way that his country house did. At the same time it should show some deference to neighbouring buildings. The relationship need not be as geometrical a one as was maintained between the houses in the eighteenth-century street; but the "apparent absence of a plan" in Tunbridge Wells, and the haphazard building in Brixton, both fell far short of the minimum semblance of order which the Regency architect expected. In exactly what form *rus in urbe* was to be established was a question to which Regency architects never managed to find a comprehensive answer, but in the course of pursuing the ideal they discovered many significant forms of planning. Their interpretations of the ideal range between the splendid terraces and squares in Islington, which are little more than free adaptations of the eighteenth-century square, and such romantic versions of it as the little group of houses known as "Park Village West" (132, 133), overlooking the Regent's Canal, in which an assortment of towered and battlemented houses are approached by way of a "serpentine" road. There are a host of variations on similar themes, most of them producing their effect by combining the informality of the landscape garden with the geometry of the Georgian town. In these layouts no consistent method of design is apparent, but certain "principles" are tacitly accepted. For example, it is noticeable that buildings are being freed from the influence of the road. The "street" as such obviously had no place in the landscaped housing estate, and architects were beginning to realise that it was less important that houses should follow the direction of the road than that they should relate to each other. To line up houses parallel with the road was coming to be considered an equally "incorrect" taste as to plant avenues flanking the drive through the park. The new function of the road, as of the drive, was to provide a series of viewpoints from which to study the compositions woven round it. This tendency to free the house from the road is mentioned because it represents a practical contribution made by Regency architects to landscape planning. Many of the best architectural qualities of the Regency town have been ruled out of the modern "garden city" because its architects have failed to appreciate the importance of this principle.

In the Regency town we are almost always conscious of moving within a space which has been organised to architectural effect. Capital is consciously made of the enclosures formed between buildings and of the planting which is seldom absent to set them off. The road itself is, very properly, at a discount.

With their ideas on taste, Regency architects could not avoid considering relationships between buildings as being largely a matter of style; the Gothic vicarage, "in keeping" with the neighbouring church, is a feature of several of their pattern books. But while considerations of style influenced the appearance of housing estates to a considerable degree, they also showed a feeling for relationships between buildings as being a matter, not merely of style, but of formally enclosed spaces, which puts the work of Regency planners on a very special plane. What this feeling was, and how it related to current ideas on landscape gardening, can be seen, as clearly as anywhere, in the various projects for the layout of Regent's Park as a housing estate.

As a commentary on the ideal town house of the Regency the case of Regent's Park is unique. The relative state of completeness in which the scheme exists to-day and the large-scale view it gives of the ideal Regency housing estate, are alone sufficient claims to distinction. What makes the design a specially significant one is that White, Leverton and Chawner, and Nash all made projects for the layout of the same site. Studied together their plans give an almost complete picture of the ways in which Regency architects were bringing the landscape into the town.

The story behind the three schemes is already a familiar one: how Leverton and Chawner were awarded the prize in a competition held for the layout of this area of Crown Land as a housing estate, how their project was shelved and the scheme ultimately handed over to Nash, as one of the triumvirate of architects which, after 1811, was entrusted with such building in London as had previously been the concern of the Surveyor General. The third plan, an earlier one made by the Duke of Portland's architect John White, was published beside the others in the report he made on the scheme under the title of *Some Account of the Proposed Improvement of the Western Part of London* (1815). Less familiar than these circumstances are the ideas which the different plans represent: ideas which could be elaborated into an almost complete thesis on the new forms of town layout which were being worked out.

The first of the projects, Leverton and Chawner's, strikes a familiar note. Leverton is generally held, on somewhat dubious authority, to have been the designer of Bedford Square, and his Regent's Park layout is an elaboration of the same system of streets and squares on the Bedford Estate which Burton and Cubitt laid out, taking Bedford Square as their model. Leverton's plan makes few acknowledgments to the Picturesque, and scarcely more to landscape layout than Burton did, although there is plenty of planted open space in the scheme. His parallel rows of houses are typical of this phase of the "green city," and it is characteristic that, even when they are formed into squares, the individuality of the blocks is maintained. This is an arrangement which avoids the planning of awkward corner houses and, as can be seen in Bedford Place, gives welcome glimpses of the gardens behind. In such features, and in the planting of open spaces on landscape principles, some deference is shown to nature as an immigrant to the town in the train of the "Man of Taste." But the scheme could hardly be called a landscaped estate in the gardener's sense of the term. The layout does not follow the lines of existing scenery. It is simply put down on top of it. Geometry dictates the lines of the plan, while nature settles meekly in the spaces allotted to her. Leverton and Chawner hardly considered the site at all. If they had done so, they must have thought twice about the effect produced by symmetrically planned squares which were higher on one side than the other.

White, in his report, considers the plan in detail from this point of view. "The principal square," he says "is so placed as to stand quite lop-sided, the second square is altogether in a bottom: and the principal lines of streets cross the summits of the ground. . . . " White's criticism that "Little attention has been paid to the levels of the land; indeed they seem hardly to have been thought of," is an entirely justifiable one, as is borne out by the appearance of the Lloyd Estate in Islington, in which a similar geometric layout stands with acute discomfort on a rising piece of ground.

White himself, as the Duke of Portland's architect, could hardly fail to be on intimate terms with the site, and this comes out clearly in his plan. A special feature is made of the crescent of houses which White describes as "taking advantage of a gradual rise of ground, which naturally favours this disposition," and which is placed so that "every house would be possessed of a complete view of the area of the crescent, and an entire command of the interior of the park." The actual effect would, however, have fallen very far short of White's description of it, for the park is so planted that every view is effectively blocked by a row of trees. To the up-to-date landscape gardener, familiar with the doctrines of Repton, this layout, with its serpentine avenues cutting up the site, must have been an abomination. That planting should be handled so that it made the most of a given area was an essential clause in the catechism of the Regency gardeners, and White's layout makes no pretence of doing so. His landscape is simply a gesture to fashion made by an architect with no knowledge of the principles which lay behind it. As such, it is, however, representative of a great deal of Regency planning. White's may not be much of a landscape, but it definitely realises that there is a place for nature in town planning, while, as in many other cases, architecture is made to suffer unnecessarily in consequence. The impressive geometry of Leverton's plan and its well-regulated succession of enclosures is reduced to a beggarly crescent, while, in the houses round the park, there is no pretence at an architectural plan. They might be said to have the last word in the argument that was encouraging the house to glory in a self-conscious "detachment," or at second best, a makeshift "semi-detachment."

Further than this it is hardly fair to compare White's plan with either Leverton's or Nash's. Both of the latter are more serious attempts at "town planning" than White's mere sketch for a "housing estate." Barracks, markets, and other necessary buildings are incorporated in these more comprehensive layouts. White uses only such decorative adjuncts as a church and what is vaguely described as a "public building." Leverton and Nash have both considered the economic side with some seriousness, while White's houses would have had to be let at princely rents to produce the semblance of an economic return. His plan is chiefly significant in showing the other element, in the form of the landscape layout, which Nash added to Leverton's design, but added to architectural effect, where White's had been merely an ineffective gesture to fashion. Mix up the best features of both the other projects and the result is Nash's. Put in more architectural terms, Nash's is a layout which has reconciled two characteristic approaches to the design of the Regency housing estate. In it the geometric layout, which is over-assertive in Leverton's and Chawner's plan and almost non-

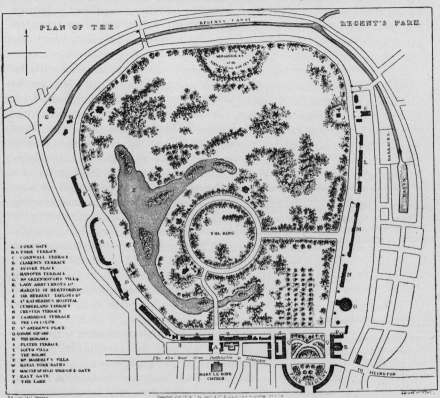

NASH'S COMPLETED PLAN OF REGENT'S PARK

existent in White's, is cleverly adapted to the landscaping into which architects were trying to transplant the town house.

Nash himself effectively describes in his report (which White incorporated in his own more comprehensive one), how he had built up his design on what, to borrow a modern phrase, might be described as the "natural aspirations" of Regency clients. "The attraction of open space, free air, and the scenery of nature, with the means and invitation of exercise on horseback, on foot and in carriages," should, he decided, "be preserved or created in Mary-le-bone Park, as allurements and motives for the wealthy part of the public to establish themselves there. . . . It is" furthermore presumed, "that those who are tempted to

build or purchase houses by the sides of dusty roads at the outlets of
the town, for the sake of looking over fields or gardens, often naked and
without trees, with the continual apprehension of those fields and gardens being also covered with buildings, and the prospects destroyed,
will prefer to establish themselves by the side of a road faced with such
dressed scenery as it is proposed to make round Mary-le-bone Park,
and which will be continually improving as the plantations flourish,
and of the view of which their houses cannot be deprived." Nash's
park can thus be considered as a permanent natural "preserve" in
which architecture is represented by a fine, flowing succession of spaces
which acknowledge geometry but do not force it on the landscape.

In their relation to the planting, the individual houses make a particularly interesting contrast to White's. They do not hover timidly on
the edge of the park, as his do, but advance boldly to take their appointed
place in the landscape. Each is, as it were, a Repton mansion in mini-
ature; all command a particular stretch of the natural scene. This idea
was modified in the course of laying out the park. Fewer houses were
built, and they are nearly all focused on the same stretch of landscape.
St. Katherine's Lodge, which is fenced off by a "belt" of trees so that
it forms a separate architectural group, is the only one of the houses in
the park which is not placed so that it commands a landscape which
falls down towards ornamental water in the approved Repton manner.

Unconsidered planting has, in the course of a century, spoiled much
of this effect. That the vandalistic tradition is being carried on is shown
by the recent planting of a row of trees in front of St. John's Lodge:
a position in which they are perfectly calculated to break the view which
Nash designed for the house. The main contours of the planting have,
however, survived a century of misunderstanding the motives of the
Regency landscape gardeners.

The estate as it was finally laid out is only a shadow of the original
project, but it is a matter for thanksgiving that Nash should have been
able to go even so far towards realising his magnificent scheme. What
is particularly lacking in it is the clear sweep of the blocks which ring
round the original layout: for "blocks" they are, and, as such much
nearer to the houses with which the eighteenth-century builder formed
his regular enclosures, than are the self-assertive "terraces" of the
ultimate Regent's Park. For it was part of the architectural make-up of
the "terrace" that it was more interested in displaying the individual
"Taste" of the architect than in assuming a dress which "went" well
with its neighbours.

Just how much freedom could be allowed in a layout of this sort was
the crucial question for the architect. The original plan is, as it were,
"given its head" in exactly the right places: in the planting and in the
means of access to the buildings, which take no more account than is
necessary of the direction of the roads. In the executed design the
buildings are more dependent on the roads and, in their design, take
less account of their neighbours. Their freedom is, architecturally

speaking, used to less worthy ends. A drive round the park to-day gives the impression of its being little more than the series of buildings overlooking a landscape which John White imagined. In the original design it was much more than this. It was an architect's promenade and not a mere scene-painter's. The buildings were part of a plan and not merely rooms behind a façade. Nash might free his buildings from many outworn conventions of planning; he could not disentangle them from their social background. For all his vision in the matter of town layout, Nash, in common with other Regency architects, was a prey to a stilted sense of values. Its hot-house aesthetics were themselves the product of a society which glorified exclusiveness as an intellectual as well as a social virtue. The gods of Regency architecture were accordingly jealous gods, and their foibles were exaggerated by the high priests of taste to impress the uninitiated.

A project such as Regent's Park could not fail to reflect some aspects of this outlook. The cult of "unlimited extent" is, for example, reflected in the shaping of the ornamental water. The disguising of its extremities by means of a combination of bridges with bushy planting is typical of the persistence of the "Man of Taste's" mumbo-jumbo in an essentially practical scheme. Above all the accent on exclusiveness, the idea that the housing estate should be a pen protecting a privileged clientele, persists in Nash's plan, and in a wider sense, builds a literal wall round the excursions of Regency architects into landscape planning. Nash's vision may have carried him over the wall at certain points, as it did when he made the Regent's Canal play a definite part in his scheme. For him it was not enough merely to use the canal as a landscape feature, with its bargees "enlivening" an aristocratic scene. He follows its course behind the scenes and elaborates the wharves and market in which it terminates into a series of squares which are calculated to make the amenities of *rus in urbe* available to a class which was seldom privileged to enjoy them. The park itself remains nevertheless an exclusive enclosure, originally intended to be accessible only to the residents and, as he suggests in his report, "those of the public to whom it may be thought proper to give keys."

Regency architects did not plan their towns for the whole community. They laid out certain parts of them for the most favoured section of the population. It follows that their planning did not begin, as most town-planning begins, with the street and with the triumphal avenue. It began with the housing estate; and often it ended with it. This fact may have imposed certain limitations on the Regency town, it certainly suggested a revolutionary approach to the whole question of town planning. For the town which begins by forcing its inhabitants into a preconceived framework of streets, necessarily subdues human interests to those of the higher authority by whom the scheme was projected. Such a plan may be made frankly to glorify a tyrannical government, as in the towns of Imperial Rome. Alternatively it may invoke the public interest, as it did ostensibly in Haussmann's "counter-revolutionary" move of turning the Paris fortifications into policing boulevards. In either case architectural effect is secured at the expense of the individual's environment. The boulevard or the public park is no real compensation for the built-up housing areas which lie behind it. Regency architects were among the first to realise the historic fallacy of the argument which said that it was. Their first concern was to make a tolerable environment for the individual, not to make an impressive setting for a crowd scene. This ambition was admittedly only realised in a limited field. Such an environment was only offered to the people who could pay handsomely for it. But for such people it was handsomely made, and, given a proper study of economic factors, such as Robert Owen's, there was nothing to prevent its being expanded indefinitely.

To be grateful to the Regency for having left us a series of well-planted town parks is thus only a superficial way of assessing the achievements of its architects. It overlooks many of their limitations and undervalues their constructive contribution to the science of making towns. Wyndham may have spoken of the parks as the "Lungs of the Metropolis": but by his one-time secretary, Humphry Repton, it was only the privileged lung that was catered for, as is shown by his fencing off the gardens of his London squares from all but the lessees of the surrounding houses. Similarly Nash may have improved immeasurably on Repton's method of laying out squares, but he still thought of the park as an exclusive "pleasure ground." Within its boundary he broke down many of the conventions which had most seriously restricted the making of a sympathetic environment in the town: but the boundary remained, and, as such, is typical of Regency planning. For, even at its most elaborate, the Regency town is not laid out as a town but as a series of housing estates, each, like Regent's Park, turning its back on its neighbours. In this it lost something of the sense of continuity which is the pride of the monumental layout. But it regained the more essential provision of free and open surroundings to the house which monumental planning forces into the background. (Hence the paradox that the consciously exclusive planning of the Regency gives us the first glimpse of the truly democratic town functioning in an industrial economy.)

Thus the Regency town began at the individual house and its surrounding layout; it did not start from the laying out of streets and public buildings. In this sense Regency architects were not born town-planners at all. Some had town planning thrust upon them by the growing sense of the town as a monument to civic prosperity, while others achieved town planning by way of more humble beginnings in the housing estate. The *fait accompli* of the completely "planned" town was seldom their ambition, and, when faced with producing such a plan, they showed a painful lack of imagination.

In working out his ideas on Picturesque layout on the Cheltenham estates Papworth eventually produced a town which, both as a work of art and as the setting for a leisurely way of life, can compare with any of the more reputable examples of the history book. But it was a very different matter when he made a preconceived layout for a complete town, as he did in his design for "Hygeia" on the banks of the Ohio. Its perfunctory "plan" is a sorry contrast to the squares and terraces of Cheltenham (50, 51, 52), growing as they do out of the conditions which the site imposes.

Interest in the housing estate did not, however, mean that the more monumental aspects of the town were entirely overlooked. The fashionable shopping centre and promenade becomes an important feature of many towns, but it comes second to the housing estate and even borrows some of its character: particularly its freedom of layout. For from the landscaped estate architects had acquired a certain disrespect for the street as the inevitable urban background, while experiments in Picturesque layout had suggested various means of breaking down its formality without losing architectural effect. The approach to Brighton is an object lesson in the Regency genius for translating grandiloquent monumental themes into more colloquial language. A less individual and imaginative architecture might have turned to the formidable avenues approaching Versailles as providing a suitable precedent for the layout. There was sufficient resemblance between the ideas behind Louis' elaborated hunting box and the Prince Regent's monster week-end cottage to suggest making use of such a plan. Another age might have done so, but not the Regency, which turned instead to that traditional feeling for designing an open space according to the lie of the land which is found in English village planning. The Brighton approach is built up from the village green: it is not, like so much street architecture of its kind, whittled down from the grand avenue approach. The central open space and its layout is given the first consideration. The buildings follow its outline so as to form an irregular background, but one which is by no means lacking in monumental effect.

This glimpse of the village green obtruding itself in so eminently "architectural" a situation reveals a *motif* which recurs in the Regency town, even outside its particular preserve in the landscaped housing estate. Admittedly architects were not above thinking of town buildings in terms of "façades," for many trends in contemporary taste were encouraging them to adopt this point of view: and to this extent they departed from the more worthy tradition of considering architecture as a formal enclosure of space. This, however, did not mean that they made the mistake, familiar in so much "monumental" planning, of treating their subjects as mere patterns on a drawing board. Quite the reverse. It was in fact a truth, which architects schooled in landscape design could not fail to appreciate, that a town must be designed from actual viewpoints five feet above the level of the ground and not from imaginary ones eighteen inches above the level of a drawing board. On the surface it might even seem that the Regency had rejected the humanist point of view of the eighteenth-century "Man of Taste," whose immediate aim was to reflect Man's pursuit of reason and order in the geometric arrangement of his buildings. But in the town, as elsewhere in Regency architecture, a fundamental humanism persists. The difference is that, instead of taking a direct view of humanity, the Regency took an oblique one: and who shall say that Man does not gain by such a change of viewpoint. Certainly his surroundings do, either when it is a question of planting a landscape to frame his country pursuits or designing an architectural background for his town life. If Regency architects failed in general to push this new humanism to a satisfactory conclusion it was largely due to the intellectual distractions which were obtruding themselves into aesthetics. They were inclined to think too much of those superficial questions of "Taste," which tended to turn their layouts into mere stage sets, and too little of their new-found freedom of layout as the structure behind a revolutionary town planning movement.

Regency architects are artists, not because of their absorption in artistic detail, but in spite of it: and the same applies in the layout of towns as in the design of individual buildings. In the housing estate they had designed settings appropriate for the "Man of Taste," attending with equal care to his views on "style" and to his delight in a Picturesque prospect: in course of which they had come upon new and significant ways of making a livable environment in the housing estate. The layout of the remainder of the town was a matter of applying these principles, so far as they were applicable, to an essentially different set of conditions. Freedom from the restrictions hitherto imposed by the street, attention to Picturesque possibilities and the principles of landscape gardening together suggested such treatments of monumental themes on a more intimite, human scale as are represented by the Cheltenham Promenade and the Brighton approach. They also fostered many adventures in the design of what was an important feature of those fashionable towns on which the Regency concentrated so much artistic effort, namely the shopping centre.

As a setting for the display of "Taste" the shopping centre suggested many variations on the theme of its providing a focus for town life set apart from the pattern of streets and squares. The arcade, with its special opportunities for showing off the "capabilities" of the glass manufacturers, was one such variation, while others ranged between the pedestrian walk at Cheltenham (2), decorated with plaster caryatids which reflect the sophisticated "Taste" considered appropriate on such an occasion, and the Crescent (125), fronted by a formal garden which formed part of the Calverley Estate at Tunbridge Wells. It is symbolical of the extent to which Regency architects derived their ideas on town planning from the housing estate that this building should have been successfully converted into a terrace of houses only ten years after it had been built.

Most of the Regency shopping centres were provided with some protection from the weather, even if it only took the form of a colonnade, such as the one which Decimus Burton designed for the sea-front at St. Leonards; and, at the same time, the idea that the more these centres were kept apart from street traffic the better, is a commonly realised one. From these points of view alone they made an impressive contribution to the town as the setting for an agreeable form of urban life. They show, above all, that it was not only in the surroundings of his house that the townsman was given freedom and space to admire Picturesque compositions among buildings, for, within their limitations, Regency architects did their best to distribute these benefits over the whole town. Such limitations, of course, included the feeling that only the more fashionable quarters were worthy of receiving the favours of

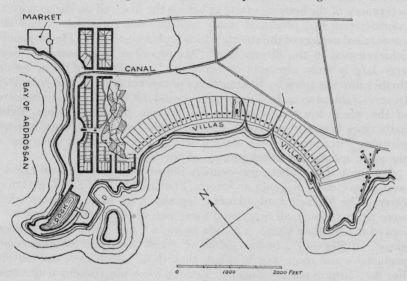

PLAN OF THE TOWN OF ARDROSSAN
P. Nicholson, Architect; Thomas Telford, Engineer.

"Taste," and also the fact that architects were tending all the time to think in terms of Estate Development rather than of laying out organically planned towns. The town of Ardrossan, in Ayrshire, which was planned by Peter Nicholson round Telford's new harbour, perhaps represents the furthest point reached by Regency architects in laying out new and homogeneous towns: and even here, Estate Development, in the form of a great crescent of houses, dominates the plan.

"Town planning," in its wider sense, did however come into its own in the remaking of existing towns. In London particularly, people were coming to consider the appearance of streets with the same critical eye with which they had become accustomed to examine the countryside. "A man of ordinary observation," says Sidney Smirke "who has had an opportunity of becoming acquainted with the principal cities of Europe, has only to walk through the streets of London, to convince himself that we are, at present, a people deplorably devoid of a taste for the Picturesque. Where, except in this country, shall we find streets of interminable length, composed of houses without cornice, architrave, or any of the most simple features of architectural decoration?"[1]

In response to the call of taste, architects accordingly applied themselves to the remodelling of the London streets in the same spirit in which they had attacked the reshaping of the countryside. The "Metropolitan Improvements" of the Regency were thus a necessary sequel to the "Improvement" of the country parks, and appropriately rounded off the transference of "Taste" from the countryside to the town. The acceptance of the housing estate as having the first call on the architect's consideration had produced many well-laid-out areas, but it had also encouraged neglect of the streets which lay between them. The Regency's achievements in the direction of "Metropolitan Improvement" came very largely from attempts to carry the "amenities" of these estates further into the town by linking them to centres of work and recreation by serviceable streets. In doing so they could not fail to become conscious of the whole town as a subject for organic planning. When higher authorities began to intervene in support of new street plans, a town-planning "movement" was started which was carried on in many of the more spectacular developments of the Victorian age.

For most of the nineteenth-century improvements in Central London were projected by Regency architects. Shaftesbury Avenue, New Oxford Street, The Victoria Embankment, together with many projects which were never realised, all originated from men who, like Smirke, had ". . . looked in vain for a Corso, a Strada mova, a Canal grande or a Herrengasse" in Regency London. Most of them form part of more comprehensive and more worthy plans than those which were carried out. For the "Improvers" of Regency London were not content with considering a street as a mere cutting through existing obstacles. They brought into play at the same time those principles of Picturesque layout which they had used to such effect in the country park and the housing estate. Nash's Regent Street (136, 137) is a case in which this affinity is particularly obvious, as it was designed with the deliberate idea of connecting Regent's Park with Westminster: while, in its design, many of the Picturesque ideas behind the park layout have been repeated. It might in fact be considered to be a mere extension of the terrace-flanked enclosure of the park. For it is less a street than a pair of theatrical façades: one to the tangle of mean streets on the East, and the other, deliberately more pretentious, to Mayfair on the West. How this idea was elaborated, the individual buildings arranged to form Picturesque compositions and the street deviated to pick up existing features such as Carlton House and All Souls' Church, has been explained by more than one of Nash's admirers. The particular point which it illustrates is the Regency planner's gift for killing whole covies of birds with one stone, in this case of using such an extravagant gesture as a grand

[1] Sidney Smirke: *Suggestions for the Improvement of the Western Part of London* (1834).

approach to a private housing estate as a means of clearing slums and bringing out existing architectural features in the town.

James Wyatt, while he had been earning for himself the name of "the Destroyer" in his cathedral restorations, had also been exploring precedents applicable to the "Improvement" of towns. He may have had to remove a belfry to do it, but he did succeed in providing Salisbury Cathedral with a reconditioned and unobstructed close from which its Picturesque effect could be properly appreciated. Similarly in the town, Regency improvements were largely a matter of bringing out buried buildings by pulling down others which had obscured them.

The Wyatt technique may not have been carried to such lengths in the city street as it was in the cathedral close. It is nevertheless the basis of much Regency improvement. To judge by the meagre plan which he made for a "Regent Street" in his capacity of Surveyor General, Wyatt himself was hardly prepared for sweeping improvements in making a street, for here he confined himself to linking up a series of existing streets, which varied considerably in width, and bringing in Golden Square to provide a certain amount of landscape relief. His project for Trafalgar Square, on the other hand, shows the methods which he had applied in the cathedral close coming into their own, with the huddle of buildings which had grown up round St. Martin's demolished and the church brought out to form a feature of the square. This suggestion of Wyatt's was followed when the square was eventually laid out, although its actual design was considerably modified, and this shows a deference to Regency initiative which is typical of the Early Victorian improvements.

Churches in general were found to provide useful monumental accents in the town plan, while they contributed to the effect of a housing estate by being made the focal point of a square. In such cases the church is often irregularly placed, as it might be on a village green, but it seldom fails to add architectural effect to the layout. Lapidge's Church of St. Peter's, Hammersmith, is a good example, as it shows how a building lying actually outside its boundaries has been brought into the composition of St. Peter's Square. Here the architect of a new housing estate is seen taking his cue from those street improvers who were freeing churches from the accumulation of buildings round them and showing them off to Picturesque advantage in the street. For example, a fire provided Papworth with the excuse for designing the opening flanked with shops which brought St. Bride's tower into the Fleet Street scene (138).

A street improvement, having as its aim the clearance of two parallel ways between the City and the West End, gave a similar opportunity for George Dance to make an ingenious elliptical clearance round St. Clement Danes, thus giving a variety of Picturesque views of the church from the widened street. Such an eye for "capabilities" had become as necessary an attribute of the street improver as of his counterpart in the landscape garden. In many Regency projects it went far towards

s

visualising a coherent town plan. Nash did not stop at revealing buried churches. He projected a "Grand Approach from Charing Cross to the British Museum" which involved incorporating the British Museum and St. George's Church, three streets away, in an open square: a plan on which Donaldson founded his embryo project for New Oxford

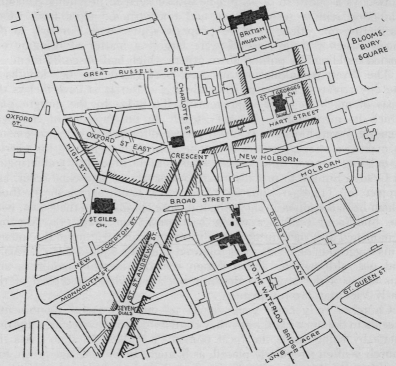

PLAN FOR AN IMPROVED COMMUNICATION BETWEEN HOLBORN AND OXFORD STREET, COMBINING WITH NASH'S GRAND APPROACH FROM CHARING CROSS TO THE BRITISH MUSUEM

Thos. Donaldson, Architect.

Street. Sidney Smirke intended to do the same for the theatres of Covent Garden and Drury Lane. They were to be linked together by a collonaded forecourt and made accessible by streets whose planning eloquently bears out his contention that ". . . a very beneficial effect will be consequent upon this purgation."[1]

Nor was it only buildings of "monumental" pretensions which in this way contributed towards a dignified city plan, for the Regency architect appreciated the scenic value of many buildings which later came to be considered unworthy of the town planner's attention. From a purely aesthetic point of view much of the most inspiring Regency architecture is found among utilitarian buildings. In such examples

[1] Sidney Smirke: *Suggestions for the Improvement of the Western Part of London*.

as the Stonehouse Victualling Yard (101, 102), designed by Sir John
Rennie, the sculpturesque approach of the architect-engineers produces
a more truly "monumental" effect than was ever achieved by the adher-
ents of taste. In such a group of buildings the Picturesque finally
comes into its own. It not only outlines their general arrangement: it
is also responsible for a sense of completeness throughout the scheme
which extends even to such details as the design of seats and lamp
standards. Here the ideas on style which generally accompanied the
Picturesque are, very creditably, subordinated to a sculpturesque
handling of the heavy stone structure.

And there are cases in which efforts were made to bring utilitarian
buildings into the town plan in a still more comprehensive way. As
surveyor to the City of London, George Dance had planned the pair
of crescents in Albert Place whose layout persists in the buildings which
have long since replaced his, and he used the same idea on a grander
scale in a project for "improving" the London docks. The fine Regency
warehouses with whose design such names as Joseph Gwilt, P. F.
Robinson and William Inwood are associated, were far from being
Picturesque objects. But under Dance's guidance, with his eye for the
Picturesque capabilities of the Monument (and not overlooking a dash
of castellation in the bridges), such buildings produce an effect which,
in Regency parlance, is more than Picturesque. It is Sublime.

The esteem in which many architects held the utilitarian tradition
was, unfortunately, to some extent at war with the dictates of the "Man
of Taste." This exclusive being might, as Payne Knight did, fully
appreciate the Picturesque aroma emanating from the "magnificent
quais of Claude," but he could not stand the more homely odour
attached to those of Billingsgate. It took a George Dance to appreciate
that one was the necessary counterpart to the other, and, at least on
paper, to show how this realisation should be acted upon. His project
gives us a glimpse of what the Regency town might have been, had its
view of "Taste" been a less limited one.

Another important aspect of the Regency town is shown in the project for a "Thames Quai," the Regency forerunner of the Victoria
Embankment. The idea, like so many others for the improvement of
London, came from John Nash, who, in his own words, dreamt of
"seeing the River Thames and its beautiful bridges made to contribute
to the magnificence of the Metropolis, instead of being shut out from
public view, behind houses, and occupied by mud-banks. . . ."[1] His
idea of "making the whole of the London side of the Thames one
continued terrace from London Bridge to Westminster Bridge" was
taken up by Colonel Trench, who, in 1824, brought before Parliament
a scheme designed by Benjamin and Philip Wyatt, with Sir John Rennie
as consulting engineer, and to which Thomas Harrison also seems to
have made some contribution. Very much an "improvement," the design
is largely the outcome of dodging existing obstacles and of turning them

[1] *Collection of Papers relating to the Thames Quay* (1827).

to Picturesque account. A built-out "pier" here, a colonnade over an
existing wharf there, make up a progression of Picturesque effects, while
a characteristic offshoot of the scheme was a project for opening up a
view of St. Paul's from the river.

It is a design which shows particularly clearly the place of Regency
improvements in the social scene; above all the suitability of adaptable,
Picturesque planning to the remaking of towns which, from the
economic point of view, were controlled by a variety of "interests."
In the actual case of the Thames Quai, Picturesque ingenuity did not
go far enough. The Temple Benchers, far from being satisfied with
a proffered view of the river from their gardens through a colonnade
"of great splendour and magnificence," claimed that their outlook
would be ruined. They joined the Strand shopkeepers, who saw a
threat to their trade in the diversion of traffic along the Embankment,
and together they sponsored a successful opposition to Colonel Trench's
Bill in Parliament.

The question of whether town planning was to be considered a public
or a private "amenity" arose again when Nash was called upon to
answer for the expense of his improvements in St. James's Park before
a Select Committee of the House of Commons. Was Carlton House
Terrace to be used as a means of public entry to the park? On this
question Nash reminded the committee that he had assumed certain
obligations to the lessees of the houses. "It must not be forgotten,"
he says, "that those gentlemen who have taken houses on the Terrace,
have taken them on the understanding that the Terrace is to be exclusively
for their use, and if a communication is permitted with the Park from
Pall Mall, I do not think it ought to be done by admitting the public
upon the Terrace, but this opening on each side can be carried through
to Pall Mall, so that if the public are admitted, they had better not be
admitted over the surface of the Terrace, but through these Arches
underneath, which would give the public all the convenience required,
and preserve the privacy of the Terrace to those who have the houses."

Nash's scheme for a private terrace with an arcade underneath it,
giving the public access to the park, is a Picturesque compromise which
is typical of Regency improvements. The monumental flight of steps
which was ultimately built is, in turn, representative of the more public-
spirited improvements of the Early Victorians. So is the Duke of York's
column, which rounds off the scheme. For the Regency started a movement for scattering monuments about its towns which finished in the
promiscuous statuary of the Victorians, and between these phases
Benjamin Wyatt's design stands half way.

The idea that the town, or more particularly the metropolis, should
reflect some of the glories of the epoch in its architecture is a recurrent
one in the years after 1814, and was accordingly incorporated in the
technique of metropolitan improvement. John White, for example,
was inspired by the thought that ". . .the commencement of this year
(1814) is perhaps one of the most memorable periods in the annals of
Britain" to put forward the idea that "some monument of the arts,

capable of impressing posterity with a sense of the dignity, opulence, and happiness of this nation, seems to be required to mark the epoch."[1] It was his own opinion, and a not unjust one, that to carry out the Regent's Park project would be the most effective way of impressing posterity, but his contemporaries were inclined to run to more monumental ideas. Smirke's projects for appropriate monuments in London, and the numerous schemes for commemorating Waterloo which were put forward before the dedication of Waterloo Bridge was decided on, represent the numerous paper schemes made for such features. The ones which materialised—the Hyde Park Screen, the Constitution Hill Arch, the Marble Arch—commemorate, if nothing else, this phase of Regency taste. But, monuments as they were, they by no means forced monumentality on the town plan.

So much of the grand manner as crept into Regency planning was derived more from existing conditions than from the town planner's initiative. The Mall is typical of this, and the layout of St. James's Park itself an adequate summary of the whole Regency approach to metropolitan improvement. An existing avenue radiating from a private mansion was here preserved as an appropriate introduction to the new palace, with a fitting formality introduced in the terraces along it, while the remainder of the park was freely landscaped. It is consistent with Regency planning that no proper entrance to the Mall should have been made and that this should have been suggested by Sidney Smirke in his more grandiose improvements of 1834. In St. James's Park, as first laid out, the Mall was in fact merely an incident in a freely planned scheme. So was the Marble Arch, as it was first projected, in the form of a pedestal for George IV's statue in front of Buckingham Palace: and it is this free planning which is so characteristic of the Regency. It is a consistent thread running through the whole of its architecture, different aspects of which have been seen in the garden, the house, the town plan; even in the planning of essentially "monumental" buildings. The nearest that architects came to realising it as a consistent aesthetic aim was in their devotion to the Picturesque. In this they overlaid it with numerous ideas which to-day seem irrelevant and many of which, persisting in a less sensitive age, proved to be definitely pernicious. Their attempts at free planning nevertheless remain as object lessons for modern architects.

Conditions have not changed sufficiently, either socially or economically, to prevent this principle from being incorporated in a contemporary architecture. The glory attached to the Gothic battlement or the Greek entablature may have departed, but the house opening to its garden, the free interiors of Soane and the open, landscaped city, remain as possibilities which have only become more desirable and more capable of realisation in the course of the last hundred years. Through glass darkened by an over-sophisticated taste the Regency, in its own way, saw an architecture with which we are now face to face.

[1] J. White: *Some Account of the Proposed Improvements of the Western Part of London.*

NASHIONAL TASTE !!!
Dedicated without permission, to the Church Commissioners —
Providence sends meat.   Parliament sends Funds —
The Devil sends cooks.   But, who sends the Architects ? _ ! ! !

From a print of 1824.
(The spire is that of All Souls, Langham Place).

INDEX

(The numbers in heavy type refer to the *figure numbers* of illustrations.)